# *Finding Your Peace Within the Chaos*

by
## Alexa Servodidio, LCSW

CCB Publishing
British Columbia, Canada

Finding Your Peace Within the Chaos

Copyright ©2016 by Alexa Servodidio, LCSW
ISBN-13   978-1-77143-270-2
First Edition

Library and Archives Canada Cataloguing in Publication
Servodidio, Alexa, 1973-, author
Finding your peace within the chaos / by Alexa Servodidio. -- First edition.
Issued in print and electronic formats.
ISBN 978-1-77143-270-2 (pbk.).--ISBN 978-1-77143-271-9 (pdf)
Additional cataloguing data available from Library and Archives Canada

Cover artwork: photo of Alexa Servodidio, LCSW by Kristin Hoebermann

Publisher:   CCB Publishing
             British Columbia, Canada
             www.ccbpublishing.com

DEDICATION

Thank you to God, my mom, dad, and brother,
for all your love and support.

Thank you, Bonnie Kaye,
for being my biggest fan and such an inspiration.

Thank you to all my listeners,
I could not have done it without you.

God Bless

# Contents

# About Alexa Servodidio

Alexa Servodidio is a Licensed Clinical Social Worker / Psychotherapist who has her own Private Practice. She works with individuals, couples, and families. Her clients are both children and adults who experience a variety of issues related to anxiety, depression, post-traumatic stress disorder (PTSD), domestic violence, sexual abuse, trauma, divorce, interpersonal relationships, communication, and relational skills.

Ms. Servodidio has a Bachelor of Science from Pace University and a Master of Social Work from Fordham University. She has also completed a two-year Post-Graduate Program at Westchester Center for the Study of Psychoanalysis and Psychotherapy in Adult Psychotherapy and a one-year Couples Therapy Intensive Program. She hosts her own radio show, Insight into Healing, which airs Wednesdays at 8pm EST on BlogTalkRadio. Blogtalkradio.com/alexas29. Ms. Servodidio explores case studies and takes questions from her listeners. *The Journal News* has also interviewed her regarding a sexual abuse scandal.

In addition, Ms. Servodidio hosts her own internet television show; The Alexa Show on alexatvshow.com. She has over fifteen years of experience acting on stage, television and in films. Find out more here:

## http://alexaservodidio.com/

# Introduction

Hi everyone and welcome to *Finding Your Peace Within the Chaos* and Insight into Healing, my name is Alexa Servodidio, I am your author and your Host. Thank you so much for taking the time out to read my book. While I was preparing to write this book, I decided to start each chapter with a question from my radio show. My vision is to provide each reader with at least one educational tool for them to utilize and then share it with another. Giving back and paying it forward are the principles I base my book, my show, and my life on. Thanks again for joining me on this journey.

# Chapter One

## Understanding Your Teen:
## Exploring Cutting vs. Suicide

"Dear Insight into Healing: Why would my thirteen-year-old daughter cut herself on purpose, something she has been doing for about three months? I am very concerned."

This may be a foreign topic to most. It is hard to grasp the idea of anyone intentionally wanting to hurt themselves. However, cutting has become very prevalent in this day and age, and is an epidemic that I address within my private practice. Cutting impacts different age ranges—from young girls to teenagers—as well as young and mature adults. Cutters are looking to release the pain, whether it is emotional or physical.

What I have found is that many who purposely cut themselves have a feeling of helplessness or lack of control over their bodies, their thoughts, behaviors, or even the way others treat them. With that in mind, it is necessary to find out what is going on in this young girl's life. Some possibilities to look at would be to ask if there is any physical or sexual abuse. Or does one suspect an eating disorder? Is she being bullied by someone? What is this person trying to escape from? Often, not always, these things can go hand in hand, so it would be prudent to research these possibilities. Social media would be a good place to begin. In the early teen years, is when one really tries to find their identity, their sense of self. Friends and social circles are what define them. I don't suggest invading anyone's privacy; however, if someone's safety is compromised, it may be necessary to check this person's Facebook page or Twitter account. It may offer answers that require immediate action on your part.

There is the question, is cutting a form of suicide or does it lead to suicide? Cutting is not usually a suicidal act, but if one does it too many times, there's the danger that any vein may get cut and dire consequences can occur. Some may try to tell you that this person is simply trying to get attention or being manipulative, but it is important, as a Parent, not to ignore it. It is necessary to begin treatment and have a psychiatric evaluation and suicide risk assessment conducted. What is triggering this behavior? I always say, "Safety first."

Cutting among friends, has become increasingly common, much like an epidemic. As we all know, kids are very impressionable and parents can become very frustrated with the choices they make. Unfortunately, just telling your child they should not be cutting themselves isn't usually enough. Without hysteria, it is necessary to explain the dangers involved when cutting with one's peers. If they are sharing cutting implements, they risk contracting serious diseases, like hepatitis or HIV. It is important to open up the lines of communication and listen. Questions to ask your child/teen would be: Why do you feel like cutting yourself? What do you gain from it? What is she trying to get through? Is she using this as a coping mechanism, perhaps to deal with stress? The concern is with that, is if they start using this at such a young age, it can manifest into her maladaptive approach to dealing with stress as she gets older.

In my practice, I have a few clients who have been cutting most of their lives. They are now in their forties and fifties. They stop for a while, but if something stressful comes up, it triggers their impulse to cut again. It may not be as deep as it was when they were younger, but it is still very serious. Not only that, it can leave scars. (Look for signs on wrists, arms, inner thighs, and the stomach, too.)

Cutting begins as a way to help one distract the mind and push away the issue that makes them feel out of control, but then it can becomes a habit. So, when I am told that a thirteen-year old girl is doing this at such a young age, it causes concern and should be dealt with right away.

Many programs use cognitive behavioral therapy, or CBT[1], and also dialectical behavior therapy, DBT. DBT is a therapy designed to assist clients in identifying negative patterns of behavior that are maladaptive, such as self-mutilation, suicidal ideation, and substance abuse. Through self –regulation clients can become more aware of their triggers, while learning the coping skills to address their negative thoughts, behaviors, and emotions.

The layers must be peeled back, in order to help her explore a healthier way of handling feeling out of control. It is the start of having her take an assessment, a self-inventory, if you will, of herself and her emotions.

Anyone, whether they are this young girl or an older adult, who is using cutting as a release should be evaluated, get into therapy, and address this right away so that it doesn't become something that will follow them for the rest of their life. When you are the parent or guardian of someone you suspect is doing this, don't sweep it under the rug. Otherwise, it will only get worse.

Here is another question from a concerned mother: "I am a single mom and I have a fourteen-year-old son. He's very smart, but he seems to isolate himself a lot. I am concerned because he has begun to show aggressive tendencies toward his younger sister. What is wrong with him?"

Let's start with the isolation. It sounds like this may be something new and a changed behavior. If that is the case, I would want to know if there have been any events or triggers that caused this isolation. And, the fact that he is aggressive toward his younger sister is another red flag. The isolation and aggression are warning signs that something is going on.

Questions to ask, is he being bullied in school? Is he having academic problems? Is he having some difficulties with peers, since he is

---

[1] Type of psychotherapy in which negative patterns of thought about the self and the world are challenged in order to alter unwanted behavior patterns or treat mood disorders such as depression.

at the age where he is starting to identify with who he is? These are important questions to ask.

I would want to know just how bad it is at this point. Is he getting physical and you are frightened for your younger daughter's safety? Is this usual brother and sister pushing each other around and bickering or has it escalated to a higher level?

Trust your gut instinct, that gut feeling that something is not right. Trust it, but also sit him down and try to find out what the issue could be. Look at his grades. Talk to his teachers and school counselor. Find out if there is any acting out in school. Find out what his friends are like. Are they new friends? Are there drugs or alcohol involved?

Something else that may not have crossed the mother's mind, but something to consider—Are there any learning disabilities? Sometimes children who never have expressed any issues suddenly act out in school. They talk during class and sometimes become the class clown. Even though other people think this is funny, many times children do this as a form of distraction because they do not understand the subject. The teachers see it as bad behavior or an attempt to get attention, when it could be some form of a learning disability.

If this has been going on for a while, I would suggest taking him to your primary care doctor and finding a Psychiatrist in order for him to be evaluated. The psychiatrist will advise you on your next step of treatment, if necessary.

Perhaps, too, your son doesn't understand why he isolates himself or why he has aggressive tendencies toward his sister, which could be very frustrating and difficult for him. The two warning signs are a cry for help and something that should not be ignored.

This brings us to our next question: "My fourteen-year-old daughter is boy crazy. She doesn't pay attention in school and is always texting or on the computer with boys. I'm scared that she is sexually active. How can I stop this?"

Well, without a doubt, this is a tough time in this young girl's life and it's also a tough time for the parents. She is starting the process of becoming a woman. It is normal behavior to like boys at this age, but the mother seems to be wary that there is something more going on, that something might be a little more than normal.

Because this young girl is on the computer and texting all the time, I would suggest seeing what she is expressing, especially since you suspect she may be sexually active. Are the conversations flirtatious or conversations about what is going on in school or are they sexually based? Yes, there is a controversy about whether or not parents should check their children's emails or text messages, but sometimes it is necessary, again, for the well-being of your child.

First, sit down with her and let her know you have some concerns. Let her know that you want to know what is going on in her life and who she is talking to. If there is some sexual content, that needs to be discussed. There is a lot of sexting and sending sexual pictures to friends and something that teenagers think is fun since "everybody" is doing it. But it's a very serious matter since the body is sacred and not meant to be on social media for everyone to see. A fourteen year-old does not have the judgment or emotional growth to understand what they are doing.

Since she is not paying attention in school, what are her grades like? If she is failing, that is important to know and meeting with her teachers, as well as the school counselor, would be a good idea. This way you can find out what she's like in school. How does she act with boys, as well as, with her female peers?

Being curious about sex is one thing, but if she is over sexualized, that may be another red flag to look at. Where is that stemming from? This way it can be addressed and worked through sooner rather than later.

When you do sit down with her, find out just how boy crazy she really is. Is this an obsessive behavior, something abnormal in a fourteen year-old girl? Is she emotionally needy with these boys? Is she trying to fill a void by seeking attention from boys in order to feel good about herself?

Without a doubt, so many young girls have body image issues and feel pressure to be perfect, to be thin, to be beautiful. Is she pressured to be a certain way, acting out a certain way that is not who she is, but to gain attention and to be accepted? Take time to explore her self-esteem and find out how she feels about herself. Is there a recent change in her behavior, including her attitude, dress style, and eating habits? Is she dressing more provocative and not eating as much? Is she more aggressive? Young girls, and boys, go through a transition stage, but there is a fine line to keep an eye on.

During your conversation with her, find out if she is communicating with just one particular boy or many different boys. Does she have a boyfriend, but doesn't want you to know? Maybe she knows that your rules forbid her from dating, so she doesn't want you to know. However, even though it will be difficult to discover if she is sexually active, this is a very important conversation to have. Find out if she's being pressured to be sexually active and does it make her feel uncomfortable. Sometimes kids do things to be accepted by others, and this may be one of them.

Again, this is a difficult conversation to have, but it is one I think every parent should have with their child. It opens up communication and is important for her to know that she can come to you to discuss anything, including conversations about alcohol, drugs, or being bullied. She needs to know that there is a safe place where she can address these topics.

# Journaling Exercise

Write down an event in your life that was a turning point and why. This can be either positive or negative. How did it change your life and why?

The reason I encourage journaling, is that many times we don't realize or connect to the major life events that have happened in our childhood, that were turning points for us.

It is important to acknowledge and explore them.

# Chapter Two

# Maintaining Peer Relationships

"Dear Insight into Healing: We just moved to a new state, and now my ten-year-old daughter is having difficulty maintaining peer relationships. It seems that she defines herself by how many friends she has, but she is having difficulty making any in her new school. What can I do to help her?"

One of the best things that a parent can do to help their child in a situation like this, is to sit down with them and acknowledge that you understand just how difficult the change is. Many parents often think it is better to let things work out on their own and not say anything, especially if their child doesn't consider this an issue. However, that is where the danger starts.

First, recognizing that moving is one of life's biggest events is a good place to begin. Let your daughter know that it is an adjustment for not only her, but the whole family. Therefore, you are all in this together. Yes, you are leaving the familiarity of your previous home, school, and neighborhood and must adapt to everything new. However, when you say that your daughter is having a difficult time "maintaining" peer relationships it leads me to wonder what is going on. One needs to ask, who are the peers? What is your daughter seeking from these friendships? Is she seeking a sense of stability without knowing much about the peer?

For instance, what if someone happened to tell her they liked her shoes or her hairstyle, which to your daughter opens the door to the friendship. Does she then cling to this person who mentioned something in passing, making her appear overly eager? The major concern in this is that maybe she is not equipped to evaluate whether or not this peer would be the right kind of person with whom to hang out with. As a ten year-old, she is just beginning to form her identity and must learn how to select friends who hold the same values as her family does. Therefore, she needs an adult's guidance to learn how to pick peers who are not going to compromise her principles in any way.

My suggestion is to find out what is happening both physically and emotionally with her. Has she started her menstrual cycle yet? Is she developing breasts? If so, it is important to be sure that she knows what is occurring with her body. Then, be sure to find out what type of people she is trying to befriend and why. Ask her how they are reacting to her. What do they talk about? Is she trying to bribe them to like her? I work with a lot of young children who seem to overcompensate when they want to make friends. It is too much, too soon. They may let them "borrow" their favorite blouse or video game in hopes of maintaining that friendship. Or they may want to claim that friend as their own and want to be the center of their attention, which should be explored further.

In building your child's sense of self, find out what qualities your daughter possesses as a friend. Have her define what she brings to the table and what type of qualities she would like others to have in order to sit at her table. When I am referring to "table" I am identifying traits, morals, strengths, and characteristics. After that you will want to teach her about the importance of being a good listener and knowing what the boundaries in the friendship should be. Ask her what activities she enjoys and then find peers with the same interests.

If your daughter comes home in a bad mood, find out why. Explore with her peer interactions and outcomes. By looking at your daughter's patterns and exploring them could provide you with enough information in order to help her learn how to maintain healthy peer relationships. This isn't to say that it is easy and not upsetting, but it is necessary, since it will assist her in how she forms and maintains relationships in the future.

Also, it may be a good idea to speak to your daughter's principal or guidance counselor. They may observe behaviors that you are missing and can monitor how your daughter deals with her peers. What some adults tend to forget is that our children are often brought into situations that are difficult, but we do not see it since we are too busy juggling all of our changes. Children can adapt to so much, but they are still children and, like adults, have a breaking point. She will see how you are reacting to the new move and mirror much of your behavior, if there's any negativity. Let her know that you are in this together and will get through it together. Suggest an activity that is outside of the school curriculum. Does she like to dance or draw? Find a program or club in which she could join. Giving her options will help show her she's not forced to maintain unhealthy peer relationships in a school environment.

I am not sure how often this young girl has been required to move, but I've found that with children who have moved a lot, sometimes they simply shut down, which reminds me of another listener's apprehension:

"I am very concerned about my twelve-year-old son. Due to my husband's job, we relocate every two years. I know this is a crucial time in my son's life and I am concerned that he might be suicidal. What signs should I be looking for?"

If there are any red flags or safety concerns have him evaluated immediately. I would first begin with why you think he is suicidal or has suicidal ideation. Is he showing signs of depression? Is he isolating himself? Does he have mood swings? Does he act hopeless, distant, or angry? Is he getting rid of his belongings or has he stopped participating in activities he once enjoyed?

Instead of trying to make a lot of friends, some children in this situation purposely cut their feelings off as a defense mechanism. A thought that could cross their mind is: Why get attached to someone when I will be uprooted eventually anyway? This type of negative monologue formed as a child can impact them when they get older: How will they relate to other people; to romantic interests? To work? Friends? Family? If this is what is happening, it becomes a maladaptive way of dealing with change and must be discussed. However, if a parent feels their child might do something more drastic, they need to intercede right away. Do not wait for an obvious red flag since it may be too late. Open those lines of communication right away! Say something such as, "I've noticed you've been really sad and I'd like to help you get through it." Bringing it to the forefront and letting him know you are concerned that he may be considering doing something permanent, is a good place to begin. As a parent, you cannot assume that he is being overdramatic. It is scary to think about, but something has triggered this thought in this listener's mind and it must be dealt with right away.

Since this young boy had to move so often, he may be a target for other children to bully him. This can be serious and not just a matter of kids being kids. As we see on the news and social media sites, kids take their own lives to escape from being bullied. Bringing him to be evaluated by a physician is a good start. A doctor can begin to assess the degree of depression this twelve year-old boy is experiencing. Meanwhile, it would be wise to be sure he does not have access to a weapon that could cause harm to himself and others.

Again, opening up a dialogue with him is an important place to start. Having a safety contract is essential. A safety contract will allow you to have a clearer picture of what your child is experiencing and will provide precautionary measures. A safety contract is an agreement between you and your child that he/she will not hurt themselves. If they feel triggered they agree to notify you, a professional, or a family member before acting on it. This does not mean he will be deterred from hurting himself, but is a way of assessing where he is emotionally and a means of explaining to him how serious suicidal ideation can be.

In this contract, have your child answer the following questions:

1. What makes you sad?
2. What makes you angry?
3. Do you ever feel helpless? If so, why?
4. How are you doing in school?
5. What activities do you enjoy?
6. What activities do you hate?

Once you have the answers, you will need to move on to more specific questions, such as, "How will I know when you are really upset? What would it look like to me? How will I know that it is more than just having a bad day?"

If the child has difficulty identifying or expressing these feelings, here are some of the serious signs to look for:

1.  Is he isolating?
2.  Is he refusing to talk to others?
3.  Is he is giving prized possessions away or throwing them out?
4.  Does he experience bouts of crying?
5.  Does he become easily angered?
6.  Does he fight with others all of the time?
7.  Has he accidentally or intentionally damaged property?
8.  If there is a family pet, is there signs of neglect, abuse, violence? If so, this is very serious.
9.  Do you suspect there might be substance abuse?

If he is exhibiting any of these behaviors, it is imperative to have him evaluated immediately. Other areas to explore are: How does the family as a whole deal with stress? How do you problem solve? Work with your child to build up your child's self-esteem and reinforce what there is to look forward to in the coming months. Let him know how much he means to you and as a team you will work together.

Once again, if you suspect someone is considering suicide, please put this book down and address the situation right away.

# Journaling Exercise

Write down 3 people you admire and why?
Who is each person and what characteristics do they possess that you admire?

# Chapter Three

## Domestic Violence

Domestic violence does not discriminate. Race, ethnicity, creed or income level does not deter it.

During my radio show, Insight into Healing, numerous listeners have sent in questions concerning domestic violence. Here is a specific question from a listener:

"I have been married for ten years and recently divorced by my husband. He was physically, verbally, and mentally abusive at times towards me. For some reason I can only remember the good times and I feel guilty. Is there something wrong with me?"

This is a very common question that comes up in my Private Practice and on my radio show. When ending any relationship whether there was abuse or not, is difficult, but that does not mean that the good times are automatically erased.

Often it is difficult for anyone to grasp the idea of a divorce. Recalling the good times can be a coping skill to survive, to move forward. Since that person was such a huge figure in one's life, and even though it became a toxic relationship, we begin to question. We begin to analyze everything, every statement, fight, every dinner we made, every good time that we had, in order to find that moment where we can say, "That was it. That was when *it* happened." However, it's not usually just one moment. It's a pattern of moments, a history.

For many, it is very difficult to acknowledge that they were physically, verbally and/or mentally abused. Meanwhile, this is where the healing and processing begins. A divorce is a death of a dream, a death of an ideal; a death of a relationship. And like any death, there must be a grieving process. Abuse leaves scars; physical scars, emotional scars and mental scars, which means in an abusive relationship one needs additional layers of processing and healing from the trauma. Some people may say, get back on the horse, go back out there and get over it. However that is not healthy. It takes time. It is necessary to sit with yourself, sit with these uncomfortable feelings. I understand these feelings and memories are frightening, that's why I strongly recommend anyone experiencing this to begin treatment. It's imperative to see a therapist, to try group therapy, and maybe go to a battered women's / battered men's group. When there has been abuse, it impacts the way we think, the way we feel, our judgment about ourselves, and our self-esteem. We start questioning ourselves and we need support during these difficult times. By speaking to a professional and sorting out everything, you can begin rebuilding your sense of self.

Many victims of abuse feel guilty because they remember the good times. It's important not to judge yourself, which is easier said than done. I think remembering the good times is part of the process. However, it is important not to just focus on the good times. Sometimes when we do that, we forget about all the bad situations and minimize in our own minds what actually had happened. We also sometimes try to justify what happened. "Well, maybe if I only did this better or if I was a better wife or if I lost weight or if I did this or that." It is important that you don't allow yourself to go down this path, because there is never a justification for physical abuse, verbal abuse, or mental abuse. No matter what, there's *never* a justification for it. If we try to provide excuses, it may make it seem okay and it's not. It is wrong!

Your husband was wrong for what he did to you, what he *has* done to you. There was nothing that you could have done to make him not to be abusive. That is his responsibility and what he has to process. Still, this does not mean that it is easy because there was that connection and many feel they want to help them or fix them. You try to tell yourself that your partner is a good person, even when they are abusive.

The abusive partner must take responsibility, come to an understanding that people can trigger us, but we have the decision on how we're going to react to it, how we are going to behave. We have that choice and we have that power. We have that ability. Therefore, it is a matter of getting to the point where we realize that nobody *makes* us do anything. The perpetrator of the abuse needs to take responsibility for what they have done and how they react to situations. This is really important in any relationship, even if there isn't any type of abuse.

We all have choices whenever someone upsets us, hurts our feelings, or makes us angry. We can either choose to say something vicious in return or even become physical, or we can choose to walk away. I realize that it can be difficult to do this, especially when we're in an argument, when we're in emotional turmoil. It can be a challenge to stop ourselves and say, okay, what am I doing? How am I reacting to this? How can I make this a healthier situation? It takes time and practice. Your partner needs to know there is never a justification for violence.

I mentioned being mindful of our emotions, mindful of how we react to things, mindful of our words during crisis. When people are really angry, really hurt, they are feeling vulnerable. Lashing out, saying things that are cruel and painful, words that often cannot be taken back. In many scenarios the person we love the most is the one that hurts us the most. It is necessary that the perpetrator of abuse, works on not letting themselves get to that point where they are saying vicious, horrific, below-the-belt comments, statements and attacks. It is not good for you and, obviously, not good for the other person. Nothing good comes out of it. You are not going to "win." After all, what do you win? You hurt the other person and went below the belt. You crossed the boundaries and it only adds more fuel to the fire. It is playing with life and death.

Another layer of abuse that needs to be addressed; is the grooming process. Victims are often groomed over time. It begins to chip away at one's well-being, one's self-image and one's self-esteem of who they are as a person. The victim is not really aware of what is happening. They may have a slight feeling in their gut, like this doesn't feel right, but then over time they are forced to ignore their gut instincts. Their sense of self has been shattered and they begin to question their survival.

It is important at this point to remember, there is always a way out. You are not alone.

This brings us to the second question that sheds more insight on the grooming process.

"Dear Insight into Healing: My boyfriend is very jealous. He has not hit me, but has pushed me really hard. What do I do? I really love him and this has only happened once?"

Unfortunately, I feel this will become a pattern. In my professional work I have seen this scenario one too many times. I know this listener wrote in with the best intentions and a genuine desire to work through this horrific event, but this is not for her to process alone. Her boyfriend needs to acknowledge his role, if anything, and fully comprehend the seriousness of his actions. What might start off as an impulsive act of jealousy has too many times turned into a deadly disaster. I know I am sounding harsh, but it is not to be taken lightly.

Unconditional love is often misinterpreted. It does not mean one should endure emotional, mental, verbal and physical abuse. So many times victims misconstrue their efforts to heal the relationship and "change" their significant others behavior, as unconditional love. That is why I feel sometimes society has such a hard time believing certain victims. Victims can be "stereotyped" or judged, and often shamed. I have seen this too many times. Comments like "Why didn't you leave, you must like the abuse" or what did you do that made him hit you?" ,often echoes through the grapevine. Blame has no business in this equation. It actually traumatizes the victim again and reinforces the negative monologue in their heads. This type of blanket statements really upsets me as a therapist, and reinforces the need for increased awareness for Domestic Violence.

I have seen clients who, because of domestic violence, suffer from post-traumatic stress disorder, severe anxiety and depression Therefore, this is a process and where finding a support team is a necessity. Finding a therapist and attending groups for battered women/men will allow you to start your journey to healing. Also, try not to judge yourself. Try not to look back and question what you could have done better. The goal now is to heal and rebuild your sense of self.

Remember, you are going to have a range of emotions through all of this. Sit with them and let them run their course and see how you feel in a month, two months, three months, and incorporate journaling exercises that will explore the roller coaster of emotions. Keep track where you are emotionally at different times of the day for example; morning, afternoon, at night, and keep a checklist of how you're dealing with changing emotions. Create a safe, calming, non-violent space for yourself.

That will be your foundation of finding your peace within the chaos.

# Journaling Exercise

Take a self-inventory or your emotions at different times of the day.

At the end of the day, week, or month, identify and compare your range of emotions and look for patterns and triggers. After you have completed this process, begin to develop coping skills to utilize in everyday life.

# Chapter Four

## Bipolar Disorder
## and
## Borderline Personality Disorder

"Dear Insight into Healing: I have been diagnosed with bipolar disorder since 1990. I often feel depressed and isolate myself. I am on medications, but what else can I do?"

Based on the self-report from this listener, it leads me to believe that he has seen his primary care physician or psychiatrist to obtain medication and a diagnosis. However, I am not sure if he is in therapy, since patients can obtain their medication without being seen by a therapist. I find that having both therapy and being on medication is ideal—behavior and medication management in tandem work together with great results as I have seen with many of my clients. Sometimes medication alone doesn't alleviate all of the symptoms, the feelings of isolation, the highs and the lows, and the mood swings. The medication can assist in taking the edge off. I suggest strongly also keeping a journal or checklist to see if there is a pattern or cycle of behaviors. This will provide you with a monitoring system of your moods.

Clients can tend to have a cycle that may run every three to six months or can be triggered by an anniversary or holiday .When this occurs, the mood swings can increase. Rate your moods from one to ten. One for depression is I am okay, I feel an underlying sadness, ten on the other hand, is when you are isolating yourself and feeling very depressed, having suicidal ideations. At this point, you should seek professional help immediately. If one is feeling suicidal or having suicide ideations, therapy is imperative and your primary care physician or psychiatrist must be informed right away. Going to your local emergency room is necessary. Having suicidal ideation on a constant basis at a high degree is dangerous, where you must seek professional help. There should be a team involved, monitoring your emotions and safety. Again, it's always a matter of being safe.

Transitioning to the mania, "one" can be "I feel excited, with possible racing thoughts, but I am able to manage my impulses. A "ten" would be engaging in risky behaviors, the sleep cycle would be completely interrupted and you would feel like a racing car without brakes.

There is also National Alliance on Mental Illness (NAMI).[2] NAMI provides a variety of programs. They have different meetings and groups—everything from anger management, budgeting, how to advocate for yourself and how to function on a daily basis. They provide a support system so you don't feel like you are alone. By being involved, it is providing you with tools on how to manage your moods and developing coping skills to enhance your quality of life. It is important to build a schedule. A schedule gives you purpose and guidelines for daily living. When you isolate, you tend to deprive yourself of positive reinforcement and interaction with others. Depression can increase, which can lead to low self-esteem and distorted thinking.

Journaling is another essential tool. Journaling is a way we communicate how we are feeling. Sometimes we cannot understand what is going on with us, but by writing it down and looking at it later in the day, week or even several months later, you start to notice a different mindset. It can provide you with a better insight of what and how you were feeling at that time, and it may identify the triggers. Are there certain things that trigger your depression, that trigger you to isolate, trigger your mania? A journal in my professional opinion can be considered a way to take a self-inventory of your moods and behavior.

It is a matter of making a lifestyle change. Being aware of what's going on in your life, who you allow in your life, what you allow in my life. You will want to surround yourself with healthy, positive people, because you need that team to keep moving forward.

Let's move on to the next question:

---

[2] https://www.nami.org/

"Dear Insight into Healing: I was recently diagnosed with borderline personality disorder. I feel very concerned and confused. What can I do to live a normal life?"

There are the different criteria that are in the DSM-V that outline what Borderline Personality Disorder is. Since this listener has been diagnosed with it, it may be concerning and confusing to him because the diagnosis can be so overwhelming. No matter if it is a mental illness, diabetes, or another medical condition, it takes a while to sit with it and process it. Sit with the confusion and the concerns and be sure that you are not blaming yourself or anyone else. You didn't do anything wrong. Educating yourself about Borderline Personality Disorder and treatment options can improve your quality of life.

Seeing a therapist, going to a day program will allow you to develop skills of self-regulation, regulation of your mood and your feelings. For instance, many with borderline personality disorder feel empty and bored. They attach themselves strongly to others, but then become intensely angered or hostile when they believe they are being ignored or abandoned by those that they depend on. It is important to be aware of these feelings. Are these relationships out of desperation of being accepted, of having someone there? In addition, it is important to be aware of healthy relationships too.

Without a doubt, this is very, very difficult. I have worked with many clients with borderline personality who have intense feelings of abandonment, anger and sadness. They also carry the burden of guilt of wanting to know why they feel the way they feel. Why am I so intense? Why do I attack those I love?

I would also like to take a moment to address those who have family members or are dating someone with borderline personality. It is true that sometimes their behaviors are very hurtful. They're very dangerous and can be threatening—things that they have said and done are really damaging. I am not excusing dangerous, abusive or illegal behavior, but they are acting out usually because of their desperation. They are so overwhelmed with the feeling of abandonment, of feeling ignored, not feeling loved, that they go to these different extremes of emotional instability. They act out behaviors to try to satisfy or fill a void. As a family member or loved one of someone with borderline personality, it is so difficult and you may often wonder why is this person so vicious to me and attacking me, when I've been so good to them. This is when you need to remember that this is something that comes with the disease. They sometimes experience brief psychotic episodes, which may resolve very quickly or take some time.

Getting involved in a program, which many hospitals and clinics offer, will help. There are many programs for DBT that teach and allow that person to grow while showing them how to regulate their emotions and be mindful of their states of mind.

Being present with these feelings and being aware of what triggers you, is essential in learning how to manage everyday life.

This is very important because when you begin to judge yourself, you hinder the process. Then your emotions take over and you start down that vicious spiral. You begin to get angry and that triggers the rollercoaster of the different emotions. Therefore, being able to just look at the facts will let you see what the reality is. Do not let that negative monologue keep running. Put it to the side and look only at the facts. Let this be a new day! Look at it with new eyes.

Take a step back and accept it while not feeling a need to react to it. You don't have to make it better. You don't have to fix it. You don't have to punish the person. You don't have to try and stop that person from leaving or hurt them. Just sit with it and see where to go from there.

Even for someone who doesn't have borderline personality, this can be difficult. But if it's applied to our everyday life, it puts things in perspective. It really makes sense of how many times we let ourselves run away with this story in our head, when it might not be the right narrative. It might not be the reality. This isn't to say we won't find some truth in it somewhere, but then do we run with it? Do we run with our story? No, that isn't our story. Yes, it is affecting us, but let's gather all the facts before we do run with the story. It is important to regulate your emotions so your mind won't be racing with all these different thoughts because that could trigger more anxiety.

However, by focusing on the action that you are doing in each moment and being in that moment, you're allowing yourself to be present. You're not being distracted by other things that are going on, by past thoughts, by past actions. Instead, you are sticking with the moment. You're in reality.

I do an exercise with clients who suffer from anxiety and severe panic attacks. If they feel like they are having an attack, I have them count back from 1,000 or name every person on their favorite sports team, giving their number, stats, what they do and so on. If a negative thought or emotion intrudes, and they start to feel anxious again, they have to go back to the beginning and start from 1,000 again or from reciting their favorite team members. Therefore, if the client notices that by the time they get to 900 when counting backwards, their anxiety decreases by forty percent, they have gained a very powerful tool. They see a way out and feel hopeful. It is an important discovery to realize that their anxiety or depression is temporary and not permanent.

Each situation is different. Use the tools you have for them. Don't consider the situation from the previous week and compare it. Maybe the situation was similar, but remember that each situation is different. Each relationship is different. Each person is different. Each interaction with that person is different. Try not to let past behaviors, past attempts, past thoughts to come in and cloud your thoughts, cloud your emotions and take over. Focus on the truth.

We don't have to prove anyone wrong. We don't have to show someone that they hurt us. This doesn't mean you have to put up with people treating you horribly or that you should not be assertive. There is a difference between being assertive and being aggressive.

Being assertive means that you will not allow yourself to be treated badly and will not be put in a bad situation. If you choose aggression, deciding that you are going to tell that person just how horrible they are, be aware they might not be able to listen, because when emotions are high, people get into defensive mode. They really cannot hear what you're saying.

Rather, it is better to argue assertively and not aggressively. But also ask yourself if this situation is even worth arguing about. Is it worth defending? It might make more sense to just walk away from the situation.

So, when the young man asked how he could live a normal life, I suggest looking for a DBT program. See if there is any type of day program and get involved in something that is ongoing, that will help hone his skills. Learning those skills is imperative because it is possible to have a normal life.

In addition, seek a therapist. I don't know if medication had been prescribed, but it is important to consider all the different avenues available and become as educated about borderline personality as you can. Read a lot of information. Consider what the National Alliance on Mental Illness has to offer since they are in every state and offer a number of different groups.

It is very powerful to give back, to be able to teach people from what you've learned how to manage, how to heal, how to process. Later on when you feel in a better place, being able to provide help to someone who is suffering, too, can be so rewarding and very helpful to you, as well as, to others.

# Journaling Exercise

This one is called the Personal Enhancement Journaling Exercise.

Step one: Do something for yourself that encourages you to accept yourself. For example, when you get out of the shower, write "I love myself" on the foggy mirror.

Step two: Help someone out. For example, shovel your elderly neighbor's driveway, if it has snowed.

Step three: Reconnect with a positive person from your past or work toward meeting new ones.

# Chapter Five

## Keeping Those Resolutions

"Dear Insight into Healing: Every New Year's I make a resolution. And within three months, I'm back to my old ways. What do you recommend and how can I succeed?"

Does this sound familiar to you? Well, you and this listener are not alone.

People make big goals for their New Year's resolutions and even think about them throughout the year. I'm going to stop smoking. I'm going to lose forty pounds. I'm going to start exercising. I'm going to do this. I'm going to do that. Then they wait for this one moment when it is going to happen and everything is going to change on that one day… or the next day… after they made this resolution. Since I am also a certified personal trainer and aerobics instructor, what I find that works from these New Year's resolutions is that the goals should be small, achievable goals. Losing thirty pounds in one or two months is not only unhealthy, but not feasible. It would be better to start going to the gym once or twice a week and doing at least fifteen minutes of cardio instead of attempting something that is less likely to be attainable.

You may think doing something on a smaller scale is not going to do much. I'm not going to lose thirty pounds right away! But it is not about quick results. It is about learning long-term healthy behaviors in order to sustain long-term results. Anything that happens "overnight" usually doesn't last, it doesn't stick.

It is a matter of taking those little steps. It is something that needs to be planned and not a spontaneous gesture right before the New Year. Instead, you must ask yourself, how did I prepare for this? What tools have I set up? What support systems have I set up? If you haven't done any of these things, quite likely, even if you made these resolutions with the best of intentions, you will become upset and disappointed in yourself. You wonder why you cannot just get it done. After all, you make the same resolution each year, but ask, why can't I just accomplish it?

It is a lot harder than just saying, this is what you are going to do without preparing yourself mentally, emotionally, and physically. You have to look at it as a lifestyle change. You must make this an everyday commitment to being a healthy person. Sometimes it is confusing because people don't realize that this is something that they have to think about on a daily basis. However, it doesn't mean that it is going to consume everything that you do; not at all.

It is like anything. In the beginning, you must be aware of your triggers, your thoughts. Be aware of your behaviors and start to adjust them. You're not going to get rid of them completely, but learn how to id patterns. You cannot just get rid of something completely and not have anything to replace it; otherwise it is a void. This is why I think it is important to plan throughout the year.

For instance, if you want to lose weight, consult with your doctor first. Thinking about cutting out unhealthy carbs and start going to the gym. Instead of getting that ice cream every day after work, maybe cut it down to twice a week. It is about starting with little lifestyle changes.

Once you accomplish those, you begin to feel better. You start feeling a sense of satisfaction and your self -esteem has improved. Be mindful not to be too hard on yourself. You do not want to set yourself up to fail. So why sabotage yourself? You're not in competition with yourself.

Remember, the habit or behavior you really want to change or adjust didn't occur overnight. Therefore, you cannot get rid of it overnight. It takes time, like anything, to work through it and to be able to ask, what did this serve for me?

I work with many people who have had addictions: smoking, eating, alcohol, or drugs, and I ask them, "What was your relationship with food? With cigarettes? What about alcohol or heroin? What do they mean to you?"

Their response is interesting, since they realize that these addictions were almost like an unhealthy friend to them. Therefore, it is as though they mourn the loss of that drug, food, or behavior that served them.

So then we must explore further because emotions can be irrational. Did you use it when you were bored? Was it a means to make you feel comforted? Did that drink or cigarette make you feel good? Did you think of them as rewards for one reason or another? These are important questions to ask and it requires being honest with yourself. Why did you use that? What was your personality like when you did? What did it do for you? How did you see that person, event, or cigarette? Once you are able to define what it served for you, you can begin to find better ways to take care of yourself when you are triggered. You can find a better reward instead of having that cigarette, ice cream or glass of wine.

Consider going for a walk or eating a protein bar. Implement healthier behaviors, but don't give yourself huge goals in a short amount of time. Make sure that you can work on something every day to accomplish that goal. Prepare your mindset. Be sure you have support from those around you. Be aware of how you're feeling, what your emotions are, what your needs are, what your strengths are, and what your weaknesses are. This will give you a better picture of what these behaviors served in your life and help you to reach that goal!

Earlier I mentioned avoiding having toxic people in your life, which reminds me of this listener's question:

"Dear Insight into Healing: My best friend is extremely negative. She puts me down and is always criticizing my dreams. Should I end the friendship?"

That is another very difficult question that I hear a lot. Is the best friend attacking her personally when she is criticizing her dreams and does she even know that she's doing this? Sometimes people who are negative don't realize what they are doing. In turn, friends excuse the behavior and just put up with it. They believe the best friend has good intentions and doesn't mean to be cruel—it is just how they are.

I understand that to a degree, but to be criticized all the time can be damaging. No matter what type of person you are or how strong you are when someone is constantly saying negative things to you, it becomes a sense of brainwashing. You can't do it. You can't do it. You can't do it. You begin to believe this and it is like verbal, emotional, and mental abuse. At first, if the person says it, you might dismiss it and think it is just their opinion, but you are human. After hearing it over and over again, it starts to eat away at you. You begin to ask yourself, what is this all about? After all, this is supposedly your best friend. What do you get out of the friendship? What does this friend bring to the table? Why are you staying in this friendship? Has it been something going on for a long time? Do you feel guilty and think you need to fix them? Or do they simply have full reign?

My suggestion is to sit down with this friend and let them know just how negative they are being. They may think it is constructive criticism. There is a fine line between constructive criticism and abuse. If I feel that the behavior is wrong and inappropriate, I will be assertive and will set boundaries, telling the person not to speak to me in such a negative way, but will do so constructively.

Of course, if this best friend is scared for her friend's safety and is worried, that is something else. Maybe the friend is on drugs or in an abusive relationship and the best friend is genuinely concerned. However, attacking and putting down this friend will not work. Nothing good can come from that. Instead, if this best friend is really concerned, she should approach it from a place of kindness and support. It is always the best avenue to take.

So, to respond to this listener's question, I would have a heart-to-heart talk with the best friend. Let them know that you are not comfortable with what the best friend is saying. Tell them, "If you're concerned about me, that is fine, but I'm okay. Let's just be friends and move forward. Your commentary is offensive."

After you have set the boundaries and your pain has been expressed, if the best friend says she cannot deal with that and will always say how she feels, then the listener has to ask herself just how important is this person in her life. If she decides to keep the friendship, but the best friend still chooses to keep doing what she's always been doing, the question must be asked, is she really a best friend? Is this someone healthy to have in her life? Where is the encouragement and support? If they are not providing that, I would take a step back and ask why do you need this person in your life? It is important to put yourself first in situations like this, especially if you're feeling this person is being vicious and negative all the time. That does nothing positive in your life. Instead, choose people who are supportive. This doesn't mean being like a Pollyanna without being realistic. It is a matter of finding that middle ground.

This brings to mind Jeanine Finelli, a guest I had on my show. Jeanine wrote the book, *Love Yourself to Health...with Gusto! Toxic Relationships, Toxic Food, Toxic Thoughts...No More!* Here are some of the topics we discussed about growth:

Church: It is a beautiful thing when people grow their faith. It is important to surround yourself with a healthy and positive team; a network of friends, family, colleagues and mate. This will be essential in developing your sense of self and maintaining it through the chaos.

Unplug: Turn off the cell phone and sit quietly outside. Why this is so powerful is the fact that we all live to learn, and be okay with being alone with ourselves. We need to sit in the silence, the uncomfortable feelings and allow ourselves to process our pain. Always finding a distraction is a quick fix that will only end up proving to be a disaster later in life. We cannot push our feelings, thoughts, and emotions under the rug. They need to be acknowledged and embraced. That is why it is so detrimental not to have toxic people around you. You are setting yourself up for disappointment. They will not hear you and you must disconnect yourself from them.

Zip it: There were countless times when I would engage rationally with an irrational person. Choose to stay away from the three ring circus and get on with your day. Here is a good place to once again suggest journaling. Write down your thoughts each day and then at the end of the week, check in with yourself emotionally, mentally, and physically. Rate your quality of life. Write down your barriers and strengths. Really explore all those different emotions, moods and behaviors. It is a self-inventory.

Feeling anxious sometimes causes physical ailments, including stomachaches and headaches. Being in tune with your emotions gives you strength and power over what is going on in your life. And, remember not to judge yourself. Do not write how badly you handled something, but rather look at yourself and decide what needs adjusting.

# Journaling Exercise

Write down your thoughts each day and then at the end of the week, check in with yourself emotionally, mentally, spiritually, and physically. Rate your quality of life. Write down your barriers and strengths. Really explore all those different emotions, moods and behaviors. It is a self-inventory

# Chapter Six

## Couples Therapy:
## Infidelity Barriers and Lack of Intimacy

"Dear Insight into Healing: I have been married for four years and have two children. I recently caught my husband texting an ex-girlfriend. I am distraught. Is my marriage over? Will I ever be able to look at him again the same way? What did I do wrong? I am in such shock!"

I've worked with many couples where there has been infidelity and also where there has been texts being exchanged with someone who could be considered a threat to the relationship. This has caused conflict within the marriage. One person feels blindsided and so traumatized that it can become overwhelming. However, to answer the question, is my marriage over, is up to each partner. Is this something that they can work through and are they both willing to commit to trying to repair their marriage?

After working with a number of couples, many who thought prior to the infidelity that they wouldn't ever consider giving their partner a second chance. However, when it actually did happen, it shook them to their core and made them really wonder if they wanted to end their marriage. Therefore, what I usually do is work with the couple and try to identify what was going on in the marriage before the infidelity, texting, or outreach to the third party occurred, and discern if there were any warning signs, including a lack of communication.

Not that it is an excuse to ever cheat on your spouse or significant other, but sometimes there are things that build up and there are some red flags. However, we must take the time to really look at what has transpired. What I have found is that even if there is no infidelity in the relationship, there still may be the lack of communication or a need to improve on the way the couple interacts with each other, and couples therapy[3] will address that.

Now, I find that most couples have kind of a dance, meaning that they go back and forth, which is a cycle of how they communicate, and how they get through the day. One might be the pursuer, one might be the distancer, and they go back and forth with these roles. They often reenact something out of their childhood, something that they did not resolve or something they'd witnessed within their parents' marriage. Whether it is conscious or subconscious, they bring it into their present relationship.

If a child is witnessing chaos, abuse, trauma, addiction, it is difficult not to personalize what is happening, even if it has nothing to do with them. Obviously it is not the child's fault. But children, no matter what age, do know what is going on. I know a lot of people think otherwise, but I have sat with four and five year old children and they can tell you exactly what is going on. Unfortunately, though, they often take responsibility for what the parents are going through. This is why it is important to have a healthy couple's dialogue, because you are modeling for your children how they are going to communicate on their jobs, with their friends, and romantic partner. It will be beneficial for them to see how you communicate and to be able to take that and apply it to their own relationships. Mirroring[4] is an essential tool in improving your communication and listening skills. Some examples of mirroring statements are: "I heard you say you feel neglected, is that correct?" Then following that: "Did I get it? Is there more?"

Many of us have our own inner monologue, which can be from childhood. It can be positive or it can be negative, but because it is repetitive and routine, many times this monologue just comes up and

---

[3] *Short Term Couples Therapy The Imago Model In Action*, second edition, by Wade Luquet Foreword by Harville Hendrix 2007, Routledge Taylor and Francis Group

[4] http://www.relationshipjourney.com/dialoguetipsdawn.html
MIRRORING means repeating back your partner's words so you both know you have actually heard the Sender's words. Both the Sender and the Receiver have responsibilities during Mirroring.

takes over. Many times we're not even aware of it, which can skew how you are actually listening and hearing. So when your partner is talking to you, being able to put aside your own emotional feelings as you are listening, as you are hearing the content, can strengthen the relationship.

As a therapist, we are trained to listen without judgement. It takes time to learn to listen in this manner, because it is different than having lunch with your friend and listening to how their day was. You are listening with different intent. Being able to know what your intent is, when you're listening to your partner, it is a matter of focusing on the goal and not on who is right or wrong. Being able to acknowledge, listen, and hear are the essential steps in moving forward.

This doesn't mean that you compromise or give up how you are feeling or that you have to agree with what they are saying. And by acknowledging what they are saying does not mean that you are enabling the behavior or that you are losing an argument. Remember, everyone needs to have their feelings acknowledged while understanding that emotions can be irrational. So there might not be an exact reason why a person feels a certain way, so try and listen without judgement. You become somewhat of a third party or mediator listening, even though this is the relationship in which you're involved in. Then you can repeat exactly what you heard them say. For instance, "You don't like it when I raise my voice when I speak. Or, if I'm hearing you correctly, it's really upsetting to you when I raise my voice."

Now the issue has been put on the table, so that the other person feels safe to respond, "Yes, when you do raise your voice, it does upset me and that is exactly what I'm trying to say." Now there is really no miscommunication or different view of what is going on. Once that has been clarified, the question could be asked, "Is there more?" That allows the person a platform to expose what is going on with their feelings that can be communicated to their partner without feeling defensive.

Feeling defensive is a common reaction which can cause a couple to fall into a downward spiral. This is understandable because discussing sensitive topics can make one feel very vulnerable, and it is difficult to allow yourself to feel vulnerable without a defense. In turn, you raise your voice or become angry to protect yourself. However, if the couple can agree that they have the same intent to love each other, to have the marriage work, and to be healthy with the best of intentions, it is a good foundation to move forward. This way the next time something comes up, you won't necessarily have to agree, but can listen to each other, and identify each partner's intentions.

During further exploration, acting out behaviors, such as, the control or manipulation out of fear, out of anxiety, out of anger, might surface from childhood. Perhaps it is how they saw their parents communicate so the family dynamics become second nature for them and that is what marriage looks like to them.

With that in mind, it's important to be aware of childhood and family dynamics. What was their childhood like? How did they grow up? What was every day like in their household? How did they learn to listen to each other? How did they know if they were listened to? The reason I believe these are really important questions are because they give insight into what it was like for that person growing up as a child. It gives a picture of the family dynamic.

I have been asked before, what does that have to do with anything? That was something that happened in their childhood and obviously it didn't work then, why would they bring it to another relationship?

I have found in my work with couples that each partner may reenact what happened from the past in order to get a better understanding of the present and sometimes it can provide closure. I find that people often search for this idealized closure and it's very painful because they find themselves repeating behaviors again and again, hoping to achieve a better outcome. Closure begins from within. With that in mind, until you sit with what you're struggling with, and, again, starting with awareness, only then can you work toward closure.

Remember, though, with closure, just as there is with grief, each case is different and there is no time limit on it. Some people get closure within a few months while others have been in therapy for many years and haven't gotten the complete closure they feel they need. Their growth and healing have moved at a slower pace. It is also important not to blame yourself if the healing isn't moving as quickly as you would like. It is a process, but some people want to get over it quickly, they want to work on it fast, but when that doesn't happen, they wonder what is wrong with them. Why can't I get past this? But there really is no quick fix.

Quick fixes never last. Rather, going in to acknowledge, to learn, and to grow is something that should be the focus. It is not about who is right and who is wrong or who "wins" the battle. To heal and grow requires work in order to save the relationship.

Another area for exploration is each partner's childhood. It is a very powerful journey that I have found that when I work with couples, it can also be a trigger. Many couples at this point just break down in tears since there was something in their childhood that they did not get or something traumatic happened that they were never allowed to discuss. Some even felt why bring it up since it was so long ago. Yet, that is why it is so important to give that platform to the other person. It also builds respect in the relationship where the partner is able to be vulnerable in a safe environment.

As a therapist, I create a safe space for my clients to allow them to explore their marriage and set future goals. I also outline the ground rules and boundaries. I instruct them that there isn't to be any name calling and encourage them not to raise their voices—even though it can sometimes get heated and people do raise their voices. I understand that, but there is to be no threats or intimidating the other partner. In addition, no manipulating or dominating behaviors, but to use the time to explore what is going on in the relationship. When there is anger, it can be frightening to the partner, but when the anger is expressed in a safe place and safe way, it can be processed. My goal is to teach the couple to move forward and to be able to self-regulate, which is powerful. However, this takes time, but is worth it.

The motivation is to be able to be in a relationship with your significant other and be able to discuss topics that you both agree and disagree with, but are able to hear and acknowledge each other's feelings and respect them, even if you do not agree with them—you have your opinion and they have theirs. Each person came into the relationship with their own viewpoints and inner monologues, and they cannot just be ripped away. Even if it they are unhealthy monologues, or defense mechanisms. We cannot rip those apart and leave the person with nothing. At some point in their life, these defense mechanisms served a purpose. Therefore, being able to acknowledge each person's inner monologue, coping mechanisms, and defense mechanisms, while exploring what they were used for and how they served the person. Then agreeing that it is not healthy anymore to use those same coping skills, as they grow emotionally, physically and mentally, is necessary in order to move forward. Therefore, let's see how we can combine the different viewpoints and make them their own as a couple.

So, your coping skills and defense mechanisms have to grow into healthier ways of communicating. When two adults in a relationship learn that on their own, and then learn it together, they are able to support each other and show empathy—that is, giving the other person support and strength in a healthy way. This can empower the couple.

Even though you can still argue with that person and not agree with them, you become partners as you grow. And as we think about the husband who was caught texting his ex-girlfriend, he must admit to what is going on and be honest about it. This can be difficult, but it is important not to keep any secrets and he must answer the question, can we move forward?

If the answer is I don't know, okay. Then you do not have a definitive reply. However, if the answer is definitely not, that is a deal breaker since one partner does not want to work on the marriage and it becomes a different story. But if both partners are ambivalent or not sure that this is something that can be healed, it could still be worked on. Having the agreement that they are not ready yet to throw in the towel while willing enough to work with each other and move forward is important. The wife, however, did ask, how can I ever look at him again the same?

I understand her question. I've had couples where there has been infidelity and it is hard to look at the partner in the same way prior to the painful discovery. They feel they have been violated and betrayed. This is someone they loved and trusted, and when they are blindsided, it is shocking and causes anxiety. There also can be impulsive behaviors, such as, becoming hyper vigilant and wanting to know where that person is twenty-four hours a day and checking their phone on a frequent basis. Yet, this is not a way to spend the rest of your life.

Always having to keep tabs on him or her and checking their phone is a hard way to live and is not healthy. The response may be, how will I ever know? What happens if he's doing this behind my back for so long and he still keeps doing it and then I don't know about it? Sooner or later, something will come out, and if it doesn't, it's a matter of working through it. But if you don't have some basic agreement or trust to move forward, this behavior is going to be hard to work with so that the marriage can be healed.

This is not implying that you will be comfortable with the partner going out with their friends and you won't worry. No, this takes time—and, again, there is no certain time limit. Each case is different. Instead, it is being able to take a personal inventory of yourself and ask yourself what you can work on and what is in your control. We cannot control other people's behaviors, no matter if we keep them in the house, have their phone and watch everything they do. That is not going to bring you the closure or to the place where you want to be. Being able to find that healthy spot in yourself and say, if this person, my significant other, is going to do this again, that is his action. He does this because it is about him.

That may be difficult to grasp, since there may be the feeling, if I cooked better, lost weight, or dressed nicer, he wouldn't have reached out to that third party. Yes, all those things can add to a marriage and enhance the sex life, but if they are reaching out to this other person, there is something going on with them. It may be poor self-esteem and a desire for getting more attention, which doesn't mean you are not giving them that attention. This is when opening up a dialogue to share what is on their mind becomes very important.

As part of the dialogue, they need to explore what they had visualized what marriage would be like; what would their spouse be like? How would they be spending their life? How would their life look like after five years of marriage? Ten years of marriage? Twenty? Oftentimes, reality is far different than what was visualized. Television programs show that everybody is happy or issues get solved by the time the show ends. There is a sex life that is wild and everything is going really well, including the communication, but television has created an idealization while realistic day-to-day lives can be stressful. People are tired.

Exploring one's reality compared to what is the ideal and what is the in between is something a couple can do. What would they want? What could they both agree on as a healthy way that their marriage could be?

However, I also understand that it can be difficult to put aside for a moment your personal injury, vulnerability, and to listen and acknowledge your partner's pain. This can be difficult because you have to take responsibility for your behavior. This isn't about assigning blame or punishing; this is about each person being aware of their role in the conflict or infidelity. There are two people in this relationship and each person has to see what their role is, what is going on, and being able to look at it without placing blame and judging.

When children are involved, it is often difficult to find some time alone or to afford a babysitter, the parents are tired and involved with their children's activities. But, this is where the work comes in. You have to make time as a couple, even if it is a matter of going out for a cup of coffee or for a walk where you can have an adult conversation. Don't assume she knows how much you respect her as a mother and don't assume he knows how much you respect what he does at his job. Rather, remember to tell each other often how grateful you are for what the partner is doing. Yes, people are so busy that they overlook these things or assume the other knows, but take the time to tell each other, even if you have to remind yourself with a note. It provides an opportunity to focus on the positive and not the negative.

Another reason for this is that when you do have a disagreement, there isn't the feeling of always being picked on or disapproved of. I can never do anything right. Therefore, if you get in the habit of complimenting each other, when an issue arises, they already know that you approve of them. Without the compliments and appreciation, people who have been married for twenty years are surprised to learn that their partner questions whether they love them or not because they do not show it in any way. Therefore, ask your significant other, do you feel that I appreciate you enough? If not, what would you like to hear from me? This isn't to start a fight, but a personal inventory to improve the marriage.

With many couples, when there is conflict or infidelity, intimacy is lacking, so the couple must learn how to rebuild. Many people would say at this point, the last thing I want to do is be intimate with my partner, after I caught them texting their ex-girlfriend. Initiating intimacy can be a gradual process and feel uncomfortable at first. It's important to nurture the emotional growth, the mental growth, and personal growth, in order to rekindle the physical intimacy—the touching and holding hands. It doesn't always have to be sexual. When couples put too much pressure on what the sex should be like or how often to have it, it takes out the intimacy.

Even if you have been with someone for a long time, you must work on the intimacy. You have to grow and work on it every day. It could be just holding hands more, or hugging each other more. At first it may feel forced, but it's about finding that connection, the emotional and mental connection, and then putting it into physical action. It's a representation of your commitment to each other. If there is a conflict or infidelity, it is a way of making sure to rebuild the physical. Sex doesn't define a marriage, but when something is not right in the intimacy department, it can turn into a real hindrance and block future growth.

So moving forward, remember to laugh together, do things together, and explore ideas together. This will create a stronger bond, which will lead to a healthier marriage.

# Journaling Exercise

Write down 5 attributes that your partner possesses. Share each trait with your partner. Let each partner take a turn.

# Chapter Seven

# Anxiety and Grounding

Anxiety can be such a crippling disorder. I think that is where a lot of people go wrong. They underestimate the power of anxiety and the effect it can have over one's life. On the other hand, anxiety can be easily treated in my professional view. Each case is different and should not be looked upon as the same m. o. for each person. Through CBT and medication, if deemed necessary by a psychiatrist, anxiety can be managed. When a client first contacts me about anxiety I like to explore origin, onset, triggers, length, and degree of symptoms. By doing this, I start to put together the pieces of the puzzle.

As months went by questions about anxiety were flooding my inbox. I decided to take 2 cases concerning anxiety and explore the similarities and differences. Anxiety can manifest itself in many ways. It can impact ones' sleep, appetite, and mood. Fits of rage and insomnia are symptoms that may be present or feelings of utter powerlessness and a paralyzing fear. This chapter will explore two case studies, both addressing anxiety in two different ways in two different people. It is imperative that each case be viewed as unique and have a customized treatment plan.

My first case study is a thirty-two-year-old woman, divorced with two young girls. She just started her own business and reports that her panic attacks began about three weeks prior and only occur right before she goes to sleep every night.

My next case is a twenty-four-year-old single male who works in fashion. He has panic attacks on a daily basis, especially when he is at work. His anxiety has manifested through anger. He has frequent outbursts, which results in his termination. So his anxiety is now preventing him from finding another job.

Both cases deal with anxiety, however the way the anxiety is expressed is different. Let's begin with the female who is just starting a new business. In order to get a better of idea of what is going on, I needed to know what had been going on in her life during the last six months. Even though the panic attacks may have only recently started, I like to look further back than just three weeks earlier. For instance, I'd like to know if there had been any traumatic events or any big life changes. The woman mentioned that she was divorced, so I would need to know if it was recent. I would then want to know if it was an amicable divorce or one with animosity. Did she give herself time to grieve? A divorce is a death of a relationship, a death of a dream and a death of an ideal, so one needs to mourn the loss of it. Since there are five stages of grief, I would want to find out just what stage she is in. Is it denial, anger, bargaining, depression, or acceptance? They do not necessarily have to go in any particular order and each case is different, so I would need to explore just where she is in the process.

So, I already see two big events: divorce and starting a business. In addition, she has two young daughters. Some of these events in her life are positive, but they can still cause anxiety.

The panic attacks happen before she's trying to sleep. Exploring her bedtime routine and what transpires before sleep is essential. Sometimes we are not aware of what we are thinking and it can be racing thoughts with the inner monologue that's repeating itself in our heads. Therefore, as mentioned in previous chapters, keeping a journal is a very helpful way to keep track of our thoughts. By asking herself questions and writing down the answers, it will offer her insight into her thought process. Is she worried about starting a new business? Is she struggling with having gotten divorced? Is she worried about her children?

Sometimes people have a mental list of what they've done during that day and then make a list of what they want to accomplish the following day. It is great to be able to mentally organize what you want to do the next day; however, before you go to sleep you want to be sure you're not charging your mind up because it could increase anxiety. I

have to get this done. I have to get that done. Instead of going into re-
laxed sleep mode, you are ramping it up. Not only are you thinking
about what needs to get done, but different ways of how you're going
to get things done.

My suggestion is two hours before you go to bed, write down what
you've done during the day and then what you need to do the next day.
Then about an hour later when the children are hopefully asleep, sit in
your bed without the television on so that the house is quiet. Make it
like a ritual before you to go sleep to start training your body so that
your mind will start telling itself that it is time to wind down. When
my clients come in with anxiety, we discuss mind over matter. The
mind is a tricky thing. It's a brilliant machine and can be very powerful. Your thoughts are very powerful. Therefore, being aware of what
you are thinking about when you go to bed is also very powerful,
which is why I suggest taking the time to first write down what you've
done and what you plan to do and then being immersed in quietness. I
have been told by clients that they don't have time, telling me that they
don't have the luxury of being able to have quiet time for an hour.
What I then suggest, is an established and frequently used exercise,
which is called grounding.[5]

When you are very upset, grounding will allow you to detach
yourself from the emotions, by giving you more of an objective view.
This way you have a better handle over your feelings. This is also a
matter of training yourself that this is a safe place to be. Many of my
clients find that their anxiety is so overwhelming and crippling. Therefore, by utilizing grounding, you are able to take yourself outside of
the anxiety and say, "This doesn't define me. This isn't me. I am not
the anxiety." And once you see the anxiety for what it is, you begin to
get your power back.

Grounding is a great tool that can be utilized whenever it is needed. No matter if you are at work or on public transportation and something or someone causes you anxiety, you can use grounding without
feeling embarrassed or intimidated.

---

[5] *Detaching From Emotional Pain*, Guilford Press, NY, from: Najavits. LM " Seeking Safety " A Treatment Manual For PTSD and Substance Abuse (in Press)

At this juncture, I would like to talk about Subjective Unit of Distress, or SUDS. SUDS is a tool that measures the anxiety levels of an individual. Therefore, number one would mean that there is no anxiety, and there is no depression, or anger. While ten would be that the individual is out of control with really high anxiety. You could take your personal inventory by using this scale. At one point, you may think what you are experiencing is very overwhelming and you give yourself a ten. However, as you continue to utilize the grounding techniques with the different types of exercises, you may be able to adjust that number down to a nine. This will give you the confidence to see that there is light at the end of the tunnel.

Sometimes anxiety can last all day or it comes and goes in spurts without knowing when it is going to hit. This can cause one to isolate themselves because they don't know if, when or where the anxiety will happen. They worry that they will be in a public place when they begin to feel anxious, which causes them to panic as they wonder what will happen next, all feeding into the anxiety. It is hard to prepare yourself in life for everything, which, in turn, causes anxiety. This is why grounding is such a helpful tool that can be taken anywhere. Keeping that scale from one to ten and trying to do it every couple of hours or however often you need to do your grounding exercises will help keep your eyes open. The point is, you want to be in touch with what is going on. The present. You are going to breathe through the moment. You are not going to think about the past. You are not going to let your mind drift back to the beginning or to the future, wondering what will happen. You are going to say, "I'm right here, I'm right now, and I'm going to start breathing and I'm going to start trying to calm down.

Again, we're going to start reading your mood, where you were before the anxiety began and after. You will try not to have any judgment because you do not want any negativity around you. Stay focused, simple and concise.

Let's proceed to case study #2, the twenty-four-year-old single man who works in fashion and lost his job due to his panic attacks and anger. He was screaming at his co-workers in meetings and also when someone would disagree with him. He would become so upset that he would storm out of the room. His anxiety was so high, at a ten, that he went into the fight or flight mode. He looked at it as if having to defend and protect himself. We need to explore when the anger happens for this young man. It obviously happened at work, which is a major trigger. But when else does this happen? In order to find out, he will need to look back to his childhood and examine the roles his parents, grandparents and friends played in his life as a model for behavior. How did they express their anger? How did someone react when someone was angry with them? This is important to explore in order to uncover how certain emotions were tolerated and processed. In many cases, anger and/or anxiety are not acceptable emotions to possess. Many families choose to ignore these feelings and not acknowledge them. Feelings need to be acknowledged and validated in a safe manner in order to grow as a person. Some may have been healthy while others were not.

In addition, I have found with some of the clients who have grown up in a house where there's been substance abuse, either drugs or alcohol, there is a lot of anger and anxiety. When there isn't any consistency it is difficult for a child to feel safe. As a child growing up, you need a safe environment where you are able to explore who you are, explore your interests and figure out who you will become. Do you like to play with dolls? Do you like to play baseball or football? For those who haven't grown up in a safe environment, they may experience attachment issues and safety concerns. In turn, they become blurred and, in turn, they are not encouraged to explore who they are and do not develop in a healthy sense of self, in many cases.

This is why it is necessary to explore the anger issues and find out how long this twenty-four year old man has been dealing with them. I encourage both the young woman and man to write down some of the issues that might trigger their anger and do this prior to doing the grounding, in addition to therapy. This way they will be more aware of what is going on.

Now, here are ways to start the mental grounding. Take diaphragmatic breaths, in through the nose and out the mouth, and look around your current setting Be certain you are not hyperventilating This can be done before going to bed at night, or before you go into a meeting or when you are about to do something that causes you stress. Look around the room, taking in deep breaths, breathing slowly. Start looking at the ceiling. Is it white? Then look at the floor. What color is it? Now, begin engaging all five senses: smell, touch, sight, feeling, and hearing. Don't rush through this. If you have the time, take twenty to thirty minutes. You can even take longer, if you find that this is really something you enjoy doing. Describe objects, sounds, textures, colors, smells, and shapes. By doing this you will begin to detach yourself from the anxiety and focus your thoughts on more concrete matters. This all may sound simple, but it takes you out of the anxiety and begins building your confidence. In addition, you are slowing down your heart rate with the breathing and slowing down the racing thoughts with the mental grounding. In return, you are gaining control.

There is also another established, commonly utilized exercise that you can do, called categories. It is a game you can play with yourself. For instance, try to think of all the different types of monkeys there are, or name all the oceans, continents, different states, or different television shows. If you are a sports fan, think of the team you like and mentally think of what years it was that they won, what were their scores, how many players can you name on their team? Consider saying The Lord's Prayer, reciting or singing Bible verses, or naming the books of the Bible. I have one client who researches different breeds of dogs and cats. He finds out about their different personalities. What their strengths are and what they like to do. From where did they originate? And so on. My Mother recently utilized this technique during her MRI and listed all the books she has read, their characters, and plot. She then ranked them in order of her personal preference.

This may sound monotonous, but again, it is redirecting your focus. Many clients utilize positive affirmations. These consist of the following statements: 'I am a good person. I am good enough. I am in a safe place .There is an exit. This is considered a form of self-soothing.

While you are doing these exercises, try to do them slowly. There is no need to rush. It is true that when you are having an anxiety attack or in a fit of anger, things speed up, your heart rate is up and so you want to rush. You want to customize grounding in order to identify what works for you.

There is another portion to this called physical grounding, which is when you'll actually be feeling and touching objects around you. It could be squeezing the armrests of your chair to isolating the different muscle groups. Begin by sitting upright. Squeeze your hands, open your hands. Squeeze your feet, open your feet. Consider doing this with all your muscles. Start with your toes and wiggle one at a time. Then move up to your calf muscles. Stretch them out and push them down. Go up your legs, tightening all the muscles and then loosening them. Go to your abs. Tighten, loosen. Then move to your fingers, shoulders, roll your neck, open and close your eyes. This will increase body awareness because during anxiety, we can lose touch of what our body feels like. What we do feel is the heart racing, the heavy breathing, the sweating and sometimes the need to get to the bathroom right away. I have clients that have issues being stuck somewhere without access to a bathroom. For instance, if they are on a stalled train, it triggers their concern. But if they can use the grounding exercise, it slows them down and gives them a feeling of control.

Clients can also utilize their iPhone, iPad or iPod to listen to music when encountering any perceived triggers. They have access to a song that they can keep playing and it will calm them down. Other clients have a small spray bottle that has an aroma that soothes them. If something triggers their anxiety, they pull that little bottle from their pocket and give a quick spritz. You will be able to use coping statements, such as, this, too, shall pass. I am strong. I can handle this. I'm okay.

It is important not to allow the anxiety and anger to define you. It's not who you are. True, sometimes when it is so powerful, it can be difficult to break out of it, but remember this is temporary.

One last thought I would like to leave you with before ending this chapter. Growing up and sitting in Church listening to The Lord's Prayer I often meditated on these following lines:

"Deliver Us, Lord, from every evil, and grant us peace in our day. In your mercy, keep us free from all sin and protect us from all anxiety."

# Journaling Exercise

Write down 5 positive affirmations and recite them daily.

# Chapter Eight

# Reducing Emotional Clutter

"Dear Insight into Healing: I work fulltime as a nurse and I've been married for two years. At this point, we do not have any children, but are planning to in the future. How do I organize my cluttered life to prepare for this?"

Life takes over, and this in turn can impact how much time we put aside for the ones we love, as well for ourselves. We are so caught up in our work, school, and activities that we forget to take some time just to sit back, relax and enjoy life. Regarding this question, I know that nurses' schedules can sometimes fluctuate, from working days to working nights, which can be really hard on that person, since sleep patterns are changing. It can also be difficult for the relationship. Two people in a relationship working fulltime and with different schedules can be a tough juggling act.

My suggestion is to try to see if both husband and wife could take some time off together and plan something that they enjoy doing. This doesn't mean taking up a whole day, but maybe just going to the beach or park, or even sitting in the backyard and enjoying each other's company. Taking this time and not being distracted allows your body, mind, and soul to slow down, to regroup, and build itself up. This is why it is important to get eight to ten hours of sleep every night. That may sound like a lot and impossible to do, but it is important to take care of ourselves so that we can take care of each other. It is hard to be the best we can be without proper rest.

Since the nurse mentioned that her life was cluttered, it would be worth it to see what she can eliminate from her daily routine. For instance, some activities perhaps could be "put on the shelf" for now until things calm down. Quite likely, she wants to get everything done and not waste any time, but that can also be a danger. It can cause overload and, in turn, increase stress.

It's also important that she takes a few minutes every day, whether it is ten or twenty minutes, to sit and reflect and not think about all the things she wants to get done. She could put on some music that she likes or read a chapter in a book or passages from the Bible. This will allow the brain to unwind and reach a calm level. Always in that heightened state, running, running, running, she won't be able to take time to appreciate what she has. Being able to be present in the moment and finding gratitude in everyday life is very rewarding.

Even though she has been married for only two years, marriage always needs work. Some people think that if they get married things should work out on its own, but it doesn't. Being married is like a job, meaning you have to work at it. You have to make time to communicate and learn to compromise. A conscious effort must be made. You must make it a priority and also let your spouse know that you are a priority, as well.

Oftentimes, when each partner is working fulltime, they can come home feeling stressed. Be aware of your communication styles, while giving your partner time to de-stress. This doesn't mean that you cannot come home and share the day you had with your spouse, even if you are frustrated, because they are the someone you should be able to talk to. However, do not make your spouse your dumping ground for all of the negativity that you are feeling. Yes, you are allowed to dump some negativity, but also reinforce the positive. Look at it this way: if you have a friend who only comes to you when they are upset and dumps all their problems on you, you start to feel that you do not want to be around that person. So, in a marriage, you do not want that to happen. Yet, I've seen a lot of relationships where that is starting to occur. You expect that every time your spouse comes home, it's going to be a dumping ground, even if you had a good day. You don't want to deal with it, even though it is upsetting to see someone you love so stressed out.

So, how can you organize your clutter, including your physical, emotional and mental clutter? All three are huge areas of your life and all need to be addressed because if not it will build up and spill into every area of your life.

Sitting down with her husband and looking at all the places where the clutter exists, can allow this listener to open up a dialogue with her husband. This is similar to when we do spring cleaning. There are three piles: the to-be-tossed, the maybe keep, and the definitely keep. These would not be actual piles, but different areas of their life that they could examine. It is a process, it doesn't happen overnight and takes good communication. This becomes the foundation and also some great quality time with the spouse working together as a team. Once the clutter has been downsized, it will be easier for this husband and wife to discuss having children without feeling they are jumping in without a safety net.

# Journaling Exercise

Sit down with your partner and label 3 piles:

1. To Be Tossed
2. Maybe Keep
3. Definitely Keep

Under each pile pick 3 to 5 items and list them according to necessity.

# Chapter Nine

## Artists/Films

I had the honor of interviewing freestyle legend Judy Torres, whose career I have been following for many years. Judy is a talented and passionate performer. Her story is inspiring and continues to instill hope in the hearts of many. Her music is powerful and she uses her lyrics to touch the hearts of her fans. Her journey to fame possesses so many facets that have impact on those just beginning in the music industry and to full-blown artists.

In our interview, Judy explored her struggles with body image and the impact it had on her sense of self. She allowed my listeners to hear her vulnerability and pain. Her integrity speaks volumes that matches her talent. We also discussed the harshness of the entertainment industry at times, and the need for a strong sense of self. I believe strongly anyone embarking in the entertainment industry needs to prepare themselves emotionally, physically, mentally, and spiritually. Remember who you are and what you bring to the table. Know yourself and find your niche. Use your strengths to highlight your talent, but also embrace your weaknesses; your weaknesses don't always have to be a negative. It is important as an artist of any kind that your vulnerability, integrity, and passion always shine through. Be open and willing to embrace any obstacle that comes your way. Make it your own and believe in yourself.

One of the many amazing aspects of doing my own radio show is finding interesting guests to interview, including a local musician who had been asked to play at the Capitol Theater for a second time. The Capitol Theater is located in Port Chester, New York and has been home to many music legends, including Janis Joplin, Pat Benatar, and The Grateful Dead. Charlie Scopoletti fits in just fine with those aforementioned names by creating his own legacy of talent and giving back to the community. Through his music, he has helped raise over $100,000 for charities and has been recognized for his selfless commitment to helping others with a proclamation on naming March 7th, "Charlie Scopoletti Day" by the Port Chester mayor.

Charlie's journey started at a young age when he was diagnosed with Hodgkin's disease. During my show, we explored this painful time for Charlie and his journey to recovery. He said that it was his love for music that carried him through and spoke of his treatment at Sloan Kettering in Manhattan. During recreational therapy, Charlie was provided instruments donated by outside sources. Through the use of instruments, Charlie's recovery had a huge impact in the direction he chose for his life.

Charlie is an inspiration; a story of hope for everyone. His dedication, passion, and hard work has been his testament for success. I strongly believe he is a role model for all ages and possesses the true meaning of finding your peace within the chaos.

Another inspirational musician I had the pleasure of interviewing on my radio show, Insight into Healing, was Chris Berardo from Chris Berardo and the DesBerardos. Chris is from Silvermine, Connecticut and is another artist whose passion, talent, and dedication drove his overwhelming success. Music has been a part of his life since a young age. Paved with his magnetic energy he has been an unstoppable force. I have seen Chris and the DesBerardos perform numerous times and the enthusiasm and positivity they exude is hypnotizing. His presence is powerful and the vibe of the group transforms any venue into a performer's masterpiece.

Chris Berardo and the DesBerardos tour all over the country and are able to spread their message through their music and touch all audiences. When speaking with Chris, his humor and love for life is so powerful. He takes adversity as a challenge to push even further and uses it as his platform for success. Chris Berardo and the DesBerardos never forget their roots. They always come back to where they started and give back to their community. Their hands-on approach is commendable and what makes them stand apart from the rest. He is able to encourage you to show up for life and be yourself.

My next guest whose background I would like to share with you is Mel Novak. His acting credits alone speaks volumes for his talent, such as, his roles in Black Belt Jones, An Eye For An Eye, and Game of Death. Not only is Mel a world acclaimed actor, he is also been doing prison ministry for over 30 years. Mel's knowledge of The Word and his conviction to show those less fortunate the power of coming to Christ makes him a gift to mankind.

In speaking with Mel, we explored how important it is for each one of us to put on our shield of emotional and spiritual armor. Mel's explanation of spiritual warfare and his ministering of The Bible has saved multitudes of inmates. Mel just doesn't counsel at the prisons, he uses God's Word as a way of living. He is a walking example of a true follower of Christ. Mel's battle with near death experiences has molded him into the incredible man he is today. Mel is very active doing film work, as well as his prison ministries. I am very humbled to be able to call this inspirational role model my friend. I would recommend strongly for everyone to look at MelNovak.com and The Arsenal Prayer. God Bless.

When I think of a power duo, 2 people come to my mind, Joseph Halsey and Debra Markowitz. These 2 have worked, written, produced, directed, and starred in many films that have covered tough social justice issues. During one interview, I spoke to Joseph Halsey about his film, Choice, The Trilogy. It is a film that follows 3 different people during their last days. One part of this film addressed assisted suicide. Joseph told his story of his father's battle with ALS and the impact it had on his family. We covered a person's right to choose, "quality of life issues", and those left behind, the caretakers. Each one of these roles bring up various questions to one's right to choose to live or die when diagnosed with a terminal illness.

Joseph, Debra, and I explored in depth the painful and heartbreaking existence a person struggles with when trying to survive a terminal illness or addiction. Joseph's and Debra's respect for their characters choices encourages each one of us to really explore in depth each choice without judgement. Choice, The Trilogy and Leaving are must sees and are essential in increasing the dialogue about life and death.

# Journaling Exercise

Write down 4 adjectives that describe you:

1. Emotionally
2. Spiritually
3. Physically
4. Mentally

# Chapter Ten

# The Heroin Epidemic

The heroin epidemic has taken so many lives so quickly that it is hard to find a person who has not been impacted by it in some shape or form. I have been contacted by so many listeners, family members and mental health advocates to prepare a discussion on the heroin epidemic. On my show, I interviewed Sergeant Murray who has been working very closely with the community, parents, addicts, and law enforcement officials to educate them on how to know if you or a loved one is addicted to heroin.

I have seen in my professional life many clients who had an accident or an injury and were prescribed "painkillers" for the pain. After a while many reported feeling that they were becoming addicted. After the prescriptions were finished, they found themselves craving opioids. Many state that they would never have thought they would use drugs, nonetheless shoot heroin. These are people who haven't had a substance abuse history and have a family and a job.

This quick descent into destruction is fairly common and many times deadly. Sgt. Murray spoke about how law enforcement is modifying their approach to drug offenders. They are looking at the whole picture, not just the crime. It is about finding help for the addict beyond lockup. There are many upcoming programs that assist those addicted to heroin in obtaining in-patient rehab and developing a support team. Sgt. Murray's compassion, drive and knowledge are remarkable. He is dedicated and passionate about helping those impacted by this epidemic—whether it be the addict themselves, a loved one or a peer. Building awareness and providing education to all those involved is detrimental in saving lives. Not only does heroin addiction effect the addict and those close to them, but also every community around the world. Heroin addiction has also led to an increase in crime.

I could not address this horrific epidemic without discussing my dear colleague, Bonnie Kaye, who is a radio show host, educator, and author. Bonnie lost her daughter to heroin. Her story is told in Bonnie's book, Jennifer Needle in Her Arm: Healing from the Hell of My Daughter's Drug Addiction. Bonnie's strength and dedication in helping others is powerful. She is able to tell her painful story so that she can hopefully save another parent from going through the same hell. During one of our radio interviews, Bonnie and I discussed the importance of getting drug dealers off the streets, implementing harsher laws and sentences for known drug dealers. We also discussed the fact that there are dealers outside rehabs ready to destroy anyone's chance of hope. As a community, I am asking my readers and listeners to join this fight against heroin addiction. We, as a team can make a difference. I have faith in it.

If you or someone you know is addicted to heroin, call this toll free helpline at 1-855-DRUGFREE or log on to drugfree.org.

I have also included in this chapter, excerpts from my second interview with Sgt. Murray:

MS. SERVODIDIO: Tonight I have a returning guest Sergeant Murray. This will be part 2 of our discussion on the heroin epidemic. Unfortunately, since last time we spoke, the situation has not gotten better. There hasn't been any improvements. I brought Sergeant Murray back to provide us with some additional awareness, education, and tools on how we can fight this growing epidemic.

Welcome and thank you so much for joining us this evening.

SERGEANT MURRAY: Thanks, Alexa. Great to be back. Appreciate you having me.

MS. SERVODIDIO: Yes. Thank you. And I know we were talking before the show and unfortunately you were saying since last time we did our show, things have actually gotten worse with the heroin epidemic.

SERGEANT MURRAY: Yes, unfortunately that's absolutely true and I can only speak on behalf of what we see here in our community. And I know it's very similar and draws a lot of parallels to the neighboring communities and probably across the country. But the epidemic has worsened and I think a lot of leaders are struggling with new approaches to kind of combat the problem. And gone are the days where we're going to address it from one jurisdiction to the other. Really we need to take a regional approach to it now and get a lot more agencies and a variety of experiences involved to hopefully lessen the impact that the problem is having on each and every community.

MS. SERVODIDIO: Why do you think it's growing and growing so much at such a fast pace?

SERGEANT MURRAY: Well, one of the things is I don't believe it's been addressed the same way other narcotic problems have been addressed in communities throughout the last few decades. The cocaine problem, the crack problem, the marijuana problem, they all came onto the scene in their own way. Unfortunately the heroin problem right now is very much based on a prescription pill abuse problem that's unique to this era. And when you have experts agreeing that one in four of every heroin addict has already been addicted to prescription narcotics, it draws some interesting conclusions as to why that might have happened to begin with. And it really tells the story of why we're where we are right now.

It's also affecting an interesting age group. We're talking about kids from 18years old to their early 20's. And when the problem is hidden, there's not much that families, law enforcement, or other resources can do to help.

So I believe that as communities we can expose the problem, number one, and change the culture and how we're looking at this problem of addiction. Change the culture and how people feel about prescription medication. And then, obviously, really increase the awareness of the dangers of heroin itself.

MS. SERVODIDIO: There's a lot of shame. People don't want to talk about it. And heroin is a lot different , experimenting with heroin and being at a party and saying, all of my friends are drinking, I'm going to taste a beer or have a beer to be cool, to fit in, it is so much different. That one time you try heroin, you test it, could be the one time you become addicted for life, or two, that you overdose and die from it.

SERGEANT MURRAY: Absolutely. You know, back in the '60s and '70s, they said that heroin was very recreationally used. There wasn't so much of an addiction that was connected with heroin. Where now heroin's on the scene because almost based out of necessity where you have these addicts that are addicted to the other opiate-based pain killers and medications and they're not available to them anymore. Then the natural next step is to move towards heroin which is readily available at a fraction of the price. So that's a problem that the communities have never faced before. And it doesn't discriminate, it's everywhere.

MS. SERVODIDIO: Yes. Well, I think also for a lot of parents out there, families out there listening, to really look at how much prescription medication that they have in their house, that it could start as easily as your teen or your middle schooler trying a couple of your pain killers from getting your wisdom teeth pulled or you had a serious injury, and then them becoming addicted to it.

SERGEANT MURRAY: You're absolutely right. Right now studies say that 1 in 6 teens have used prescription drugs in order to get high or to change their mood, basically speaking on behalf of pain killers and opiate-based medications. To combat that, there are programs in place that we have here in our agencies where there's medication drop boxes. There are no questions asked and you can get rid of your medications that you otherwise would just having laying around the house. That's part of a tactic that can help us prevent teens being exposed to this type of prescription drug abuse. But it's not everything. Parents have a responsibility to teach their teens about the danger of prescription pills.

There's this whole "not in my backyard" syndrome that's going on. No one wants to believe that it is in their communities, or it is a problem facing their family. I can honestly say in my opinion that the crime problem in our community, I'd say about over 80 percent of it is directly connected to a narcotic problem. It is in your backyard. And just because you may not have children that you feel are susceptible to becoming a prescription narcotic or heroin abusers, doesn't mean that this problem isn't going to affect you. It doesn't mean your house can't get burglarized by that narcotics user who's looking to get a quick score to find their next fix. We see that every day.

We see car burglaries and house burglaries literally every single day. And most of the suspects involved are narcotics users. So it is affecting everybody. And as I mentioned before, it's one of the reasons why we need to change the way we look at this problem. We can't keep blinders on. It's really affecting all walks of life and a whole bunch of different facets of the community. So there's not necessarily one starting point. You can start with your own family. You can start with your own acknowledgment that it is a problem and do your own research.

MS. SERVODIDIO: I understand that dealers of heroin actually have something similar to a promotion package. They have their own brand, their own advertising. Many times, these names, that are on the bags are something that a middle schooler would find cute. It may look like candy or something a high school student would look at and say, wow, that's really cool. That's got a fun name. And think it's something not that serious.

SERGEANT MURRAY: Absolutely, the dealers aren't dumb. They're marking it with their own stamps. They're trying to acquire product that already is stamped a certain way. They want their users and their clients to come back for that same item based on their past experiences. Unfortunately, a lot of these individual products are what we called stepped on, or cut, or diluted, or had chemicals or other narcotics added to it that -- just because it has the same stamp on it that a user might have used, you know, two days prior doesn't mean it's the same chemical makeup. And based on your tolerance, based on what you think you know about it, and based on what you think you have in your hand right now, it could be the last time you use heroin.

And again, it gets back to not knowing exactly what's in it and, like I said, where it might have been okay for you to use two days ago and your buddy used it, and you trust who you're getting it from, it could be your last time using. They are all dangerous. They're all deadly. That's the only way to look at it.

A seasoned addict who has a tolerance built up could be using the same brand or stamp that they've used all along and they still don't know what the breakdown of that product is that they're putting in their arms, snorting, or smoking. And it could be what causes them to overdose. And I know we'll talk about Narcan in a little bit, but, you know, it's giving people a false sense of security that they can be rescued. They can be saved. And I think that's contributing to the problem as well.

MS. SERVODIDIO: Yes, because people feel like they have a safety net. If they overdose or have a bad reaction, that the Narcan will save them or bring them back.

SERGEANT MURRAY: That's exactly what's happening. And we're noticing that users are using the buddy system, so to speak, where they're with somebody's who's kind of looking over them or monitoring them where they know if they overdose they can call 911, or bring them to a medical center. They know Narcan's right around the corner and it's going to bring them back. Well, it doesn't always work that way.

It's a great life saving device, but we have to back up -- even before that and, yes, use it as a tool in our toolbox to help save lives, but also address the underlying problem which is the addiction in the first place and how we should go about reducing that and lessening the impact that that has.

MS. SERVODIDIO: Yes. Because I think that's really most of the battle, I mean it is trying to get it before the addiction starts and having some awareness, having education. I've had a lot of parents come to me and say what age do we start -- should we start in high school? You know, I don't want my child to know about it if they really don't need to. I understand it's pretty hard to start speaking about heroin, but it is necessary. As we were discussing before, third and fourth graders aren't exempt now from speaking about heroin, thinking about heroin. Thinking if they're going to their friends' house, their parents have pain killers in the cabinet. They're taking them. They're becoming addicted to them. I mean, I know it's hard to even fathom that idea but it's happening.

SERGEANT MURRAY: Well, you're right. You're right. And we're seeing it more and more, unfortunately, and the age is decreasing. The middle schoolers are who we're targeting. That's who we want to make sure they know what's going on, and their parents. We want their parents to reach out to them.

What I've seen, I don't want any other parent to have to see. And they can't be too young for you to start explaining it if you do it the right way. We need to address it and get it in the mind of the middle schoolers and their parents, it may be too late by the time they get to high school. We're seeing pill parties where there's no alcohol involved in these parties, but you do have to bring some type of a pill or a prescription medication. They're throwing them in a bowl and the kids are popping them, either to be cool, or peer pressure, or to get high, or for whatever the reason, but that could be the beginning of the downward spiral. And if they haven't been educated about the dangers in just doing that one time, it may be too late by the time they get to high school.

We are seeing that kids are getting a lot of these prescription narcotics from their parents, from their grandparents. You know, it takes a lot of guts for someone -- a possible user to go into projects, or a bad neighborhood, or housing complex to buy narcotics, but it doesn't take much thought at all to go into your grandmother's medicine cabinet and take whatever she has there.

And we see that. We see people breaking into houses, whether they know the product is there or not, but there's nothing else missing except medication. So it's changing the trend in certain crime patterns. As I mentioned before, it's connected to almost all the crime we see in our jurisdiction.

SERGEANT MURRAY: I've yet to come across someone who has said that they wanted to be addicted to heroin. However, the perception of using and abusing pain killers is still "cool". It's fun at parties. It's medication that a doctor prescribes. How bad can it be? But you don't realize that it's the same opiate-based material that you're finding in heroin. And that's why it's so easy for these addicts or the prescription pain killer abuser to turn to heroin. And then that's where the shame is involved. At a party, you don't see too many people snorting a bag of heroin together and being proud of that. With this type of addiction, there is shame involved. What we've noticed is, if your son or daughter had a brain tumor, you would go to the ends of the earth to try and find the best doctor, to get the help they need, and whatever resource you could use, whoever's going to stand out and help you. You're not afraid to ask.

However, when you find out your son or daughter is addicted to a pain killer or addicted to heroin, the number one goal seems to be you don't want your neighbors to find out. So there's a disconnect there. And I think that gets back to, again, we need to change the culture in how we look at all this. There shouldn't be shame involved. The goal should be to get these people their help and to prevent it in the first place.

Gone are the days of just making the street level arrests. They've become investigations and it's a matter of life and death, and that's the way we're looking at it now. We'd be foolish to think that we could arrest our way out of this problem. That's not what's happening and it's not our plan. Gone are the days in the 70's, and the 80's, and the 90's where someone gets pulled over and it's a user or addict, or it's someone who has a problem and they have a little cocaine on them, or they have heroin on them. We're not looking to worsen a situation for somebody. If we can help them, we're going to try and help them. And if it's something that we can use to our advantage in order to help work on the overall problem, then of course, we will.

We, again, are working backwards on this problem. We are seeing the final outcomes. We're seeing the overdoses. We're seeing the people being hurt during narcotics transactions. We're seeing the money loss, the breakups of the families, we're treating it almost reactively and we want to treat it proactively.

It breaks your heart when you knock on somebody's door because you know that their child is selling their personal belongings, and electronics, and jewelry of their parents in pawn shops because we see the pawn lists. And when we knock on the parents' door and say, "Hey, do you know your daughter just sold your high school class ring?" And they don't believe it, and when they go to look for the class ring and it's gone, then this becomes the first indication that they have received that their child had some type of a narcotic problem.

MS. SERVODIDIO: I hope that through doing this show, someone listening tonight has been able to learn something or can save someone's life from this horrific addiction.

SERGEANT MURRAY: Well, I hope so too. And I hope that the next time that you have me on, that we'll be able to report some more positive outcomes.

MS. SERVODIDIO: Yes, I was just about to say that. I was saying that the third time is a charm. I'm hoping to have you back again and to have had a huge impact and be able to report that there's been an improvement. That we have made a dent in this horrible epidemic. I want to commend you for all of the work that you're doing and your passion and dedication, it really shines through.

SERGEANT MURRAY: Well, thanks, Alexa. It's people like you that have enabled people like me to be able to try and get the message out. So I appreciate that as well and again thanks for having me.

MS. SERVODIDIO: You're welcome. And again, thank you. Have a good night and God bless.

# Journaling Exercise

Research programs in your area that work with addictions and share the information on social media.

# Chapter Eleven

## Suicide Prevention:
## An Interview with Survivor Gregg Loomis

Gregg Loomis has lived in Westchester County, New York for his entire life. He is in his mid-fifties, a husband, father of two boys, a brother-in-law, an uncle to many nieces and nephews and has owned his own business for thirty years. He lives with bipolar disorder and is a survivor of attempted suicide.

Gregg joined the Board of the Westchester Chapter of the American Foundation for Suicide Prevention, AFSP, which is the leading foundation in the fight against suicide. They fund research, create educational programs, and advocate for public policy, and support survivors of suicide loss. I had a chance to interview Gregg for my radio program, Insight into Healing, and wanted to share the discussion with my readers, since I think it is important and offers a lot of information.

ALEXA: Gregg, thank you so much for joining us.

GREGG: Thank you for having me. I really appreciate the opportunity.

ALEXA: Since you participated in a walk for suicide prevention, could you please provide some background about how you became involved?

GREGG: It's really quite a story. It was almost a sign from the universe. In my recovery, I started to exercise a lot more because I found that it was healing for me. It helped me to be with myself and think about my life. I took up running and I began to run a lot. During my lunch break I would go to this particular park where I work and I would jog around an oval duck pond there, which is just about a mile. One day I was jogging and saw this sign that advertised the Out of Darkness Walk for the American Foundation for Suicide Prevention. I wrote down their Website and went back to my office to look them up. I then told my wife that I wanted to participate in the walk. I felt that I should give back and support others after everything that I'd been through and all the support and help from friends and family and professionals I had received.

My wife and I went to the walk and by circumstance, some friends who had lost their son by suicide about a year earlier were shocked to see we were there and wanted to know why. I explained to them my years of struggling with mental illness and how I had attempted to take my own life. I also met Maria Idoni, the director of AFSP Westchester Chapter who had unfortunately lost two siblings to suicide as well. We all talked and I expressed how I was more than willing to get involved with future events, the walks and other volunteer work. Maria eventually asked me if I would like to become a member of the board of Westchester AFSP Chapter. I attended the next meeting and agreed to join and here I am today.

ALEXA: Wow. How long did it take you to build up the strength, the courage to come forward? I know with some clients I work with there is some guilt, shame, and denial. So I really commend you for coming out and being such a positive role model for so many people that suffer.

GREGG: It's been a very long journey, and was not easy. It was so very difficult and took years and years for me to come to grips with what I was suffering with and what I attempted to do. When it first happened, I guess basically it was what's normally referred to as a mental breakdown, a nervous breakdown, what is more commonly known today as a psychotic break.

I suffered severe depression and could barely work. I couldn't keep attention for more than a few minutes on anything I was doing. I slept twelve, thirteen, fourteen hours a day; sometimes I wouldn't get out of bed for two or three days. I was like a zombie. I couldn't think. I couldn't eat, and the depression was devastating to my personal and professional life.

My doctor suggested that maybe I go to a mental health clinic for an evaluation and a rest. I agreed and went to Columbia Presbyterian Hospital in White Plains. This is when I was first diagnosed as suffering with bipolar disorder. Upon hearing this I was in total denial. I got very, very angry and did everything I could to get out of there. I could not understand what was happening. They told me I was manic depressive, I actually laughed and I told them that was just not possible, I did not believe them. I honestly believed they were going to put me in a straightjacket and lock me in there for life!

Most people, when they are first diagnosed with having any kind of mood or mental disorder struggle with the diagnosis. After I was released from the hospital the mania hit. I had such severe manic episodes that all of a sudden I went from being depressed and sleeping for hours and days at a time to functioning as if I had energy to do anything. Now I didn't sleep at all. I would stay up until two in the morning and then after a couple hours of sleep I would get up at 4 am. I would go to work and be able to knock out tasks like it was just child's play *Give it to me. Give it to me. Give it to me. It'll take care of it.*

There were thoughts that I was invincible and on top of the world. Unfortunately, with that comes spending sprees. I just started buying things on line, spending thousands of dollars on things I didn't even need but thought I did The mania was actually worse than the depression, because with mania came alcohol abuse.

I started drinking all the time. When I couldn't get high enough from the drinking, I started abusing drugs. I would sometimes drink cough syrup all day to get high. It was horrible, just horrible.

Eventually I crashed back into depression and was committed to a different mental institution. Only this time the crash was so severe I had attempted to take my life. When the crash hit I felt I did not want to live anymore. I had no reason to live, I felt nobody loved me, and I also had no love for anyone, my children, my wife, family, and friends. I just felt nothing for anybody. I felt like an empty shell and no longer had reasons to live. I just felt there was absolutely nothing to live for. So I tried to overdose on medication. Luckily, I was found and brought to a hospital where I received the care that saved my life.

I went through about five, six, seven years of episodes of Manic Depression. Then the strangest thing happened. It is strange only in the way I say it because I had a stroke. Actually, in the last three years I've had a stroke, back surgery and been diagnosed with cancer. Dealing with all this I feel somehow changed me because all of a sudden I felt a new outlook on life–that life was a little more precious than I was letting myself believe or think. I suddenly had this spark that I wanted to live, I wanted to beat the cancer; I did not want to be a cancer statistic, as strange as that sounds.

After the stroke, I wanted to rehab myself back to health. I began to walk, to run, I wanted to exercise. I wanted to swim. It almost gave me a new lease on life and that is where my life turned around. I use those tools and many others, especially talking to friends, family and professionals. I cannot stress enough how important it is to not only talk to peers of people who are suffering like yourself who have a story to share, to learn from, but also talk to therapists and social workers who can guide you back from the darkness.

It is so important to talk to people who want to help, have the knowledge of how to help, and the care and the love for a fellow human being, people who just want to help them and see people recover to any extant they can, and just give them back the will to live. I cannot stress the importance to talk out your fears, emotions to bare your soul!

ALEXA: I agree with what you said to make sure you have a team, to speak to a professional, to have friends, family and go to groups or meetings and make sure that you reach out because when you're in fits of depression and mania, there's kind of isolation of being by yourself, especially when the real depression comes in. The hopelessness, helplessness and not wanting to reach out. But it really makes a huge difference to see that professional because the isolation can be very dangerous and sinks you deeper into that hole of sadness of despair.

GREGG: Absolutely. I cannot even describe in words how you feel when you are at that point. How alone you feel. How little you feel, as if you have no significance in the world, in the universe, to anybody, to yourself, it is indescribable pain! You can look out the window and it is a beautiful spring day. It is sixty-seven degrees and the sun is shining. It is just gorgeous, but you feel like it is the most dreary, rainy, dark, foggy day that you could possibly be caught in. And it's scary, it's frightful, and lonely. You feel so all alone and that's when it gets very dangerous.

You are right, it is important to talk to support groups and professionals, family members, anybody that will just take the time to listen and help and care and want to get you help.

ALEXA: Did this feeling of despair, loneliness happen slowly or quickly? I mean, did you have an idea of what was going on? Some people say that it is so overwhelming and happens quickly while others say that it is some kind of underlying doom and gloom type with looming feelings and thoughts.

GREGG: That is a hard question to answer. I don't mean to be wishy washy about it because in the midst of it, you might have days where you actually feel good and it almost seems like the depression and the sadness and the loneliness was a dream and it never happened. And then you go to bed that night, wake up the next morning and you don't want to get out of bed, you don't want to see anybody. You pull the covers over your head. You want to see darkness. You don't want to think, but the more you think, the more painful things become. So, it's different I guess for different mood disorders. I feel it could be different on how it comes on, whether it's suddenly or over a period of time. And then it could be different for each episode that you may rollercoaster with.

Sometimes it can come on like bang; it just comes on. Then other times, you start feeling, ah, here it comes,—you know it's coming and you feel it's coming, and you know you have no way to stop it. Eventually, you are going to hit that bottom again.

Then again, having talked to professionals, psychiatrists and therapists, and social workers over the years, it is determined in their opinion that I've suffered with this since I was a child. In those days, in the '60s and '70s, it wasn't recognized. My family and friends didn't recognize it. Nobody knew what it was. You would be labeled quirky or different. You know, "he's eccentric." They're weird or like a rebel because they are different. They grow their hair longer than most or wear different clothes or they get a tattoo, which was unheard of in those days. So, it is hard to answer that specifically, but I would say it took a bit of time before I really snowballed downhill and hit rock bottom. It came on a little slower, but during some episodes over the years, it came on very quickly.

75

ALEXA: And it sounds like a very frightening experience, too. When you said you have a feeling it is coming, I am sure you get anxious and worried because you don't know how to stop it. You don't know if it can be stopped, but you know what you'll be feeling, what the outcome of the episode will feel like. It must also feel lonely and helpless to know it is coming. It sounds like it may take years of practice of seeing professionals, of finding your own coping skills of exercising, reaching out to others, friends and family, to build yourself back up and build tools, coping skills, to be able to have these in your arsenal to pull out when these days pop up.

GREGG: You are so right and I couldn't have said it any better. When I was in my darkest times and, again, this is my situation since everybody's situation is different, but I think there's a basic core of symptoms in the way depression works. I'd go to work, and I'd go out to dinner with friends, I'd go to a concert. My wife and I would do things in the yard or we would spend a day out at the pool and listen to the ballgame, and watch sports on TV with my sons. They would be normal days that probably many people would say the same.

But then one day, morning, evening or afternoon, the overwhelming depression, sadness or lack of self-esteem would just start. Whether it was something I saw on TV or heard on the radio, a certain song, or if I saw something happen while I was out and about, or read something in the newspaper, I could never put my finger on what triggered it. But that is when it started to snowball and you start to think, what am I doing? Why am I here? What is this worth? What am I giving to society? What value do I have to anybody?

That starts the rollercoaster, the car starts to move. You're going up that hill and you know that the crest is coming and when it does, it's downhill from there, full speed ahead and you can do nothing to stop it. You get scared. I've cried a million tears just thinking about it, and experiencing it because you feel there's no outlet. Unfortunately, you come to the point where you feel the only outlet is to take your own life, because you can't live with the never ending pain anymore and the thought of what is to come.

Someone likened the depression to sneezing. It's as if you would sneeze all day long, every day for weeks on end and you get to the point where you just can't sneeze anymore, you just can't do it and you just want it to end. Sadly, for some, that is when they end up taking their lives and that's the most unfortunate thing because it is so avoidable, so avoidable.

You mentioned the tools that I use. I learned and started to get myself healthy. I went to a natural nutritionist and she put me on a specific diet. She had me stop eating foods that are just bad for me, that are known to affect depression, and affect your mood, your body, you can just have physical ailments that can set you off into depression, if you're prone to depression. I started working out and running and joined the Greenwich YMCA so I could use the treadmills and take exercise classes, swim in the pool. I also started doing Yoga. Yoga, for me, has been a godsend because I can concentrate on intricacy of the poses and feel the energy from the mood in the room, whether it's a private instructor or in a group setting. I feel that yoga has enlightened me so much and helped me be in control of my mind and body. I know there's no cure and sometimes I go into that yoga class and I'm as sad going in as I am when I come out after. I'm still depressed, but I push myself and I discipline myself to have to push myself to think other things, to be distracted from that sadness because I don't want to feel that way anymore.

And, I would be remiss not to mention a component that is so important to fighting depression, which is alcohol and drug abuse. I have totally, by choice, decided not to touch alcohol at all anymore. I do not drink. I do not take any type of drugs that aren't prescribed. I stay away from any substance that I can abuse, that can trigger a manic/or depressive episode. Alcohol is a depressant and for people that suffer depression, it's like gas on the fire. It is the worst thing you can possibly do and can derail any hope of recovery.

ALEXA: It becomes self-medicating.

GREGG: Yeah, I'm not advocating against alcohol by any means. There are people that drink and can handle it and are very responsible and it's not a problem. But if you suffer depression, it can be the first step down that slippery slope.

So I can't stress enough, if you can just stay away from it. I order a club soda with cranberry. It looks like a drink, but it's the best I could possibly do for myself.

ALEXA: I really appreciate how honest you are with us and the listeners and how genuine you are. You really have painted a picture of what depression is and, suicide attempts, suicide ideation; it puts a face to it. I find that people who have gone through it don't understand it, don't know why. They want a definite answer: why would I feel this way? What is it? What can I do to fix it? They want to ignore it, just go outside and enjoy the day, but it's not as easy as that and you have really explained that it's a lifestyle choice. It's an every minute, every day choice that you make that you're going to survive and going to have a better quality of live and that it is a matter of working toward it.

GREGG: Without a doubt. Listen, I'm not fooling myself or anybody else if I can't be honest about what I've gone through, what I go through, and what I feel I need to do for myself to continue to live healthy for people who care about me, including my dog who loves me very much.

All that has become important again. And it's not all of a sudden that I'm cured or that I'm better. I wake up every morning and one of the tools I use that I've taught myself, that my therapist thinks is just so wonderful, is that I wake up every morning and find a reason to live that day. Whatever it is, whatever. It could be the simplest thing. It could be that I want to read my horoscope and see what it says. It could be I want to make my wife happy today. It could be I want to go on a trip. I want to see things I've never seen before. Or, it could be I just want to make a cup of coffee and sit and enjoy that cup of coffee and live in that moment. Anything I can think of. I tell myself: get up. You have to do this because, believe me, I wake up every day and thoughts are in my head, why do I bother? Why continue this fight? And it is a fight. It's a fight every day.

Depression doesn't go away. It can't be surgically removed. It can't be fixed with medication. It can't be wished away with happy thoughts. It does not go away 24/7, so it is like you said, it's a fight every day and you have to find tools. Nothing will cure it. Yoga doesn't cure it. Happy thoughts don't cure it. Medication doesn't cure it. *Nothing* cures it. But there are tools that you can use from moment to moment, hour to hour, day to day, to help yourself want to live that day and want to feel a little bit better, even if you're feeling down.

You know what? A little bit better is better than not better at all. It's just so simple. You know, not every day is good, but there is good in every day.

ALEXA: I like that. And I think it's finding the small stuff, finding those moments of peace, having a laugh about something, just being able to allow yourself for one minute or one moment to enjoy something and to be able to treasure that and keep those moments with you; to say, okay, you know, I laughed today and that was really great and to be able to move forward. Sometimes the media, things you see on television, paints a picture of how we're supposed to be—that everybody's happy, smiling, and walking down the street. In reality, day by day we all have struggles. We all have things going on. As they say, don't judge a book by its cover. Everybody has something going on and to remember that you're not alone. Don't give up. You do matter. You do have impact.

I worked with some family members who are survivors and it's such an impact. Many times people think they could have done something. It's tough. It's such a hard legacy to leave behind, so I say, don't give up.

GREGG: Absolutely, Alexa. I like to tell myself I want to live with passion, compassion, love and service. That will help me survive this depression every day. If I can do one of those four things, two of them, three of them, or all four, every day, it brings me to the next day. It fuels me and that's what people who are struggling should know that they need to fuel that fire. They need to get angry at themselves for being angry, for being sad, for being depressed. I hate to say it but you almost have to fight yourself and then push. It's easier said than done, but I've done it. So it can be done.

Again, I try not to fool myself that tomorrow I might not wake up and be in a bad place. But that's the thing, I've learned to get help. So if people are struggling, if they feel alone and feel embarrassed by the stigma that's out there about mental illness, even though it's getting better, awareness is being brought to the forefront, they need to get help. And for people who don't understand when somebody is angry and act out, it is easy to consider the person crazy.

Well, you know what, I hate to say 'crazy,' but maybe they are. Maybe they are different. Maybe they do suffer something. So take it in stride. Cut them a break. Instead of yelling back, reach out and ask if you can help them with something. Ask them if they are feeling okay. What's the worst thing they're going to do? Tell you to mind your business! You might be surprised that they reach back and say, help me. You can help me. I need help.

It's so easy to turn away another human being or to fight them or push them away or act like they don't matter. It's a lot harder, but it's a lot more satisfying if you try to help them.

ALEXA: I think that's what you're doing and it is so amazing that you're telling your story so people can relate to it. I am sure that there are many people who can relate to it. They may be saying, I thought I was the only person that felt that way. I thought something was wrong with me or that I'm weak, or why can't I get over it myself? Why can't I just snap out of it? And you get stuck in those negative thoughts and that negative monologue and you bring yourself down.

But to be able to see that someone is going through what you're going through, it's that light at the end of the tunnel. That's what we want to make sure to see, that light at the end of the tunnel. Even if you don't believe it right away, name that light and keep your eyes on that focus, because it's very important.

Also, to help other people. I tell clients and family members that just a kind word, just to listen to someone, helps. You don't have to fix their problem, you don't have to make their pain go away. You don't have to come up with an answer, but acknowledging their pain can move mountains and can actually be the deciding choice of someone not taking their life.

GREGG: There's no doubt about it. And I can't stress enough that if you're out there and struggling and you feel alone and the people around you are not supporting you, most likely it is because they don't understand. They are scared and may be as scared as you because they don't understand what's going on. They're in denial and cannot believe that their son, daughter, husband, uncle, sister, brother, wife, friend, whomever, is suffering like this. And they don't want to believe it.

I sat in many groups where the parent's child has been diagnosed bipolar; a teenager, a preschooler or younger, or someone in their college years, and the parents just don't believe it. I mean, they come right out and say that they think the child is just acting out or looking for attention, but what I have found is that in most cases the parents are just as scared as the child and cannot believe that their child has been diagnosed with this.

Remember, when I was first diagnosed, I didn't believe them. I didn't believe a word the doctors were saying to me. I thought just because I'm in a psychiatric ward, this is what you tell people. That's what I told them. "You tell people that they're crazy because this is what you do, this is your living."

But they were not crazy. If I could go back and apologize to them for the way I acted and what I said to them, I would do that. I would absolutely apologize to them and tell them thank you so much because they probably set me on a path to saving my life.

ALEXA: That's where the mental illness has to come up on the same page as any other medical condition. It is the same reaction as when someone finds out they have cancer or diabetes, or lupus or anything serious; they go through the denial phase. It is tough for people to accept any type of diagnosis, but must be treated with empathy and tell them it is something that can be worked on and understand that it's nobody's fault. It's a matter of seeing how we can move forward and make things tolerable and utilize and develop coping skills.

GREGG: You're so right. It's a disease. It's a disease like any other disease like, MS, Cancer, Lupus, ALS, you name it. Mental illness is a disease and needs to be recognized that way, and unfortunately in our healthcare system today with its stigma, it's not recognized that way.

Insurance companies, health insurance companies don't want to cover a lot of mental illness. It's sad. There are people walking around undiagnosed and walking every day up and down the street and struggling that have not been diagnosed because nobody has been able to recognize it in them. They haven't been able to recognize it or can't go and get quality help. It's sad because these people could live much better quality of life and they don't. If someone has cancer, they can get treatment. I'm not belittling cancer by any means; I've had it. But it is the perfect example. You mentioned the Out of Darkness walk, which was phenomenal. We had 717 registered walkers. The numbers were astounding because the year before we had about 350, so it was a huge success. But then I went to the Breast Cancer walk a few weeks later for my sister-in-law, and there were about 8,000 to 9,000 people. And that is a curable and manageable disease. Mental illness is not a curable disease. So you see the imbalance of the awareness. It's just the awareness. The awareness for mental illness is nowhere near where it needs to be.

ALEXA: I agree. My dad had passed years ago from lung cancer. They're getting more research with lung cancer now, but before he passed he said, "I don't think lung cancer is sexy. There's no sexy T-shirts. I think the media's not that interested in it." But when it comes to mental illness, there's a stigma.

When I went to that walk, I was so taken back by the groups and everybody had their own T-shirts with photos and names of the people they lost. One person had two family members. There were two brothers that had both died of suicide. All these young kids whose family members were walking. It was so very powerful.

And there was silence, but there was definitely solidarity there. People are stepping out and making a difference, even in their pain and suffering. Suicide is getting more awareness from those walks, even though it's a hard topic.

GREGG: It is. It is powerful and different from most walks that you see. Because even though there are smiles and exchanges of caring and support for one another, there's also that underlying emotional sadness and hardship. You can see it on some of the people's faces— they get a moment of happiness because of the support from family and team members. They try to raise funds for AFSP through their team. There is a bond there, but yet you see the tinge, that teardrop coming down a mother's face. It's very sad.

ALEXA: You had sent me some facts about suicide and depression that I want to read: Over 38,000 people in the United States died by suicide every year; in 2010, the highest suicide rate was among people forty-five to sixty-four years old, the second highest rate occurred in those eighty-five years old and older. Currently suicide is the tenth leading cause of death in the United States. A person dies by suicide every thirteen point seven minutes in the United States. An attempt is estimated to be made once every minute.

GREGG: To me, it's sad, but it's senseless, too. It doesn't have to happen. It can be stopped. It can be abated by awareness, by support groups, and by this conversation. What you're doing is phenomenal and such a great outlet for awareness and causes a domino effect. The more people hear the message, the more they relay the message and you know how that works, it's just law of numbers.

As far as AFSP is concerned, they want to get the suicide rate down. Here are some facts: They want the suicide rate to reduce to twenty percent by 2025. And that's a great goal and saving a lot of lives. But it is amazing what you said about the attempts. It really stands out to me.

ALEXA: Yes, the cries for help and the pain.

GREGG: An attempt a minute. That is somebody crying out for help and more than likely suffers a mental disorder. Ninety percent of suicide attempts and people who die by suicide are people who suffer a mental disorder.

ALEXA: That is such an astounding number. What can we do, us the community, to help the American Foundation for Suicide Prevention? How can we contact the foundation? How can we find out about events, offer services, offer help?

GREGG: The best thing anyone can do is go to the Website, AmericanFoundationforSuicidePrevention.org. There you will find all the information that you could possibly want to read about—from suicide warning signs to coping with suicide loss; who to reach out to in order to be helped, groups where you can go. There's also information on the site about understanding suicide, what is basically the cause and why people that suffer take this action when all else fails.

There's things about advocacy and public policy and all the walks, the Out of Darkness walks, the hikes, Hike for Hope. I'm excited because May's Hike for Hope is on my birthday.

ALEXA: What a great gift.

GREGG: That's exactly it. I said, of all the gifts I could get, that's the best one. I can go help someone struggling and help raise awareness and just be there for somebody that day, that'll fulfill me. So, that's the reason I have to get up and live tomorrow and every day going forward.

But again, there's things about the research, that's where the money goes. Therefore, the best thing to me would be to go to AmericanFoundationforSuicidePrevention.org. I would not recommend surfing the Net about suicide because you will get a lot of misinformation. Unfortunately, you're going to get a lot of information that someone who's struggling might think is romanticized, so I would stay away from surfing.

If you want, go to our website. There's everything and anything you could possibly want and, if not, you can contact them.

ALEXA: In addition, people can send their questions to me at InsightIntoHealing@gmail.com. I think this is a community and an ongoing outreach where there are tools that can be accessed.

GREGG: Also, if anyone is struggling, they can always call Suicide Prevention hotline at 1-800-273-8255. The people answering those phones are wonderful and are trained in getting people to the help they need. If you just call them, they are there to listen, and if it means that they have to send professionals to help, medical services, it will be done. I can't stress it enough.

ALEXA: If you're having suicidal thoughts, it's not something to take lightly. I like to go to a scale from one to ten. One, not acting on it and ten, acting on it. Where are you on that scale? Do you have a plan? Do you have access to your plan? Have there been attempts in the past? Is there alcohol or drugs involved? Are you not enjoying activities that you usually like to do? For instance, if you used to like to go to the gym, but now you don't, why? Are you isolating yourself? I think these are big warning signs. If you or someone is feeling this, go to the emergency room or call 911 before anything happens. I always say, better safe than sorry. Remember, this does not mean that you are weak. It's a team effort. I always advocate for people to get a team since there's power in numbers. It is so amazing to have a sounding board, to speak to someone that you trust and be able to say, this is what I'm going through. We're all human, we all go through ups and downs. We're sad, we're upset, we're angry, so we should be here to support each other.

GREGG: I agree with you wholeheartedly. The theme for this talk is to seek help, please just seek help. Don't fight this yourself. You don't have to. There's no reason to and that's the biggest thing we can share. You may have anxiety; it doesn't have to be bipolar depression. It doesn't have to be manic depression. It doesn't have to be schizophrenia. It doesn't have to be suicidal thoughts. It can be something you can't help yourself with and you're feeling down and beginning to spiral.

It could be at the beginning, so seek help, ask somebody, call somebody; call that number. They'll be glad to help you. They want to see you live and see you get better and live a healthier life.

ALEXA: Greg, thank you so much. I know we've helped so many people and changed a lot of lives.

GREGG: Thank you so much, Alexa. I appreciate you giving me the opportunity and hoping that even if one life gets saved from this conversation that is better than none at all. I saw a quote on Facebook and thought it was pertinent. "Just remember, suicide does not end the chances of life getting worse. Suicide eliminates the possibility of life getting better." So if you're struggling and you have those thoughts, keep that in your mind.

ALEXA: Thank you so much and God bless.

Before this chapter comes to an end, I would like to switch gears and explore with you those left behind, after a completed suicide. The family, friends, and loved ones who are left standing in the aftermath. In the film, *Living with the Dead,* writer and producer, Christine Vartoughian, explores the story of a woman's venture through life after suicide. This film illustrates the reality of suicide and the impact it has on all involved. Her truth and vulnerability allowed the viewers an inside look into the grieving process and the journey to healing.

Through films like this, I hope it will assist in bringing up this difficult discussion of suicide and depression. Creating a safe environment for those suffering from suicidal thoughts to those affected by suicide itself. I cannot stress enough to reach out, you are not alone. Don't give up. There is always a way out.

# Journaling Exercise

Plant flowers, go to a sanctuary or church and find hope and growth. Look for examples of new life and beauty. Write down five to ten examples of new beginnings. Is it planting a new life, watching a young child or admiring how beauty is found in everything? Whatever it may be, it is wonderful to see things bloom.

# Chapter Twelve

# An Interview with Reverend Danny Garcia

In the process of doing my radio show, I have been blessed to interview many inspirational guests. This chapter will cover my interview with my mentor, my colleague, and my dear friend, Reverend Danny Garcia.

REVEREND GARCIA: You know, we are commanded to pray for our leaders and to pray for all of the people from around the world. I believe in prayer and a personal relationship with God, and more listening rather than actually talking.

ALEXA: That is such an important point: really listening and connecting to God through prayer and self-reflection instead of just talking.

REVEREND GARCIA: You know, Alexa, I can't trust myself. I have to lean on my God and His Word, His Word is life to me. I couldn't do it without him. I have gone through that, since there was a time in my life during my early years where I really didn't know God and didn't have a relationship with him. He was trying to communicate with me, but I didn't want to hear it. I was too busy doing my own thing.

ALEXA: So what do you think was the changing point for you, where it hit you that you needed to listen and connect more with God?

REVEREND GARCIA: I remember it as if it were yesterday. It was about thirty years ago. I was not a minister at that time. I was producing concerts, and into the things of man; drugs, women, you know, all those things that we think fill the void. And one day I was in my living room and using amphetamines, marijuana and other drugs and my spirit was losing its mind. I didn't understand what was going on because I'd never experienced this feeling before, but I felt that my spirit was actually leaving my body. I then experienced something called fear, fear of death. And I heard the voice from the Lord, and he said, "Which one do you choose? Life or death? You must choose now.

I know from my background in my early years of going to Catholic school that I was taught the Bible, and taught about heaven and hell. So I was afraid at that moment. I knew that if I died, I would go to hell. I believed that. And I couldn't control that feeling of my spirit leaving my body and me dying. I heard a voice say, "Which way do you choose, life or death? And that is when I screamed, "Jesus, save me!" And my spirit jumped back into my body.

My girlfriend came into the room and was a bit hysterical and concerned, so she called the paramedics. They rushed me to the hospital and shot me with all kinds of things, and for a year I was a vegetable. I couldn't walk properly. I would have to hold on to the wall or onto somebody for support.

So, after a year, I wanted to commit suicide because I didn't want to live like this. Instead of suicide, I went to church, which happened to be a Catholic church where there was a group of charismatics that prayed over me and laid hands on me. Whatever was in me, which I think was that spirit of death came out of me and the spirit of the Lord came in me. From that point my whole life had changed. It was a traumatic experience. The fear of the Lord is the beginning of wisdom and the Word also says, "Anyone that calls upon the name of Jesus will be saved." I didn't know that then. I didn't know anything. And I started to learn from that point, not just about the things of the Lord, the things that we can see, but more about the spiritual world.

ALEXA: It's such a powerful story and a powerful journey that you went on. I often have a lot of questions from listeners that are going through really dramatic, drastic changes in their life and they are at a crossroads to choose either to heal from growth or to decline and stay in addiction or stay in abuse. I feel that your story is so inspiring that it gives me the chills. It is such an amazing testament to God that it is going to help many listeners to realize that it is just calling out to God and having that faith.

Sometimes we don't see what we have faith in, but I think it's that having faith and saying, "I don't want to live like this anymore," and getting the strength from God to move forward and to start living in a healthier manner.

REVEREND GARCIA: Today, I believe He is love. In 1st Corinthians, chapter thirteen, verse four, it says that love is patient. God is definitely patient with us. Love suffers long, love is kind, and love puts the other person first before you. And it also says in the end that love conquers all. I've seen it. I've walked it throughout the world, as I have walked by foot more than 26,000 miles literally by foot around the world, five continents. I've walked in His love.

I've had people ask me, how do you communicate with people that are from different languages? It's also the language of love that everybody understands. I don't care if you've been abused, gone through different kinds of tragedies, you know when somebody really loves you because they are putting you first before themselves.

ALEXA: What inspired you to do your first walk? What year was your first walk and what was it about?

REVEREND GARCIA: That was in December 1996. I was moving to San Diego and going through a divorce. For anyone going through that they know what it is. That's like being torn apart both in the flesh, but more so in the spirit. Because when you say, "I do" you're not just saying I do to your partner, you say it to God. I was lost and my wife wanted another life. She didn't want me to be her partner and I tried to fight it. I tried everything I knew for quite some time. We were together for twenty-four years. We reached the point where she was going to get the divorce. At that point, I didn't know what to do with myself and didn't want to live anymore. So I went to San Francisco and started walking to San Diego. I just started walking. I remember that day; it was raining. I had forty-eight dollars in my pocket because I had given up everything. I went from San Francisco to Hollywood to San Diego. I really must have been crazy. I was the cause. I was the victim. I was the problem. And I was the one that needed healing.

After walking in the rain for about ten or twelve hours, I ended up at a hotel. I didn't have any credit cards. I had nothing but the forty-eight dollars, but I had a friend in San Diego who called the hotel and said he'd pay for my room. However, the manager said that his money was no good and that I was going to stay there free at the hotel's expense.

I stayed about two days, but I had friends who were Marines that wanted to help me. I wasn't in the Marine Corps at the time, but once you're a Marine, you're always a Marine. There is a brotherhood there.

ALEXA: That brings up a very great point about accepting support from others, and that a community or just that one person can be that turning point, that person to lean on, to change your struggle and make it more into a growth and give you the hope and encouragement to keep going where you're going. Some of my listeners are so caught up in what's going on that they start to isolate, and cut everybody off. I tell them that isolation starts that decline. You need to have other people around, to reach out to other people that you trust, to gain support, to have friends or family to help through the struggle. It's not something to go through alone. It doesn't mean that you're weak or you're not good enough because you can't conquer this addiction, you can't get out of this abusive relationship. We are all human and need support from each other and from God. Asking for help is not a sign of weakness. It's a sign of strength.

REVEREND GARCIA: And the Bible says that when you are at your weakest point, that is when God is strongest working. He says, "Fear not, because I'm with you. I will never leave you. I will always be with you until the end of time."

I have walked by foot around the world living that. I've come to a point that I know I'm a sinner and it's only His grace that has saved me and continues to save me physically, as well as spiritually. I'm here today, alive at sixty-nine years old. Alexa, how does a man walk around the world at sixty-nine years? How do you walk, forty, fifty miles a day? And how do you do that without taking money?

ALEXA: Through God.

REVEREND GARCIA: It was the only way. This is what safe is, when you get out of your comfort zone and you do something that you can't do because you know and trust that God can do it. When I was walking in the Capitol and praying, I started thinking about all the people that go there. The Capitol is our house, it is your house. I look at the world the way it is and see the crazies in the Middle East and immigration, and I see all these things going on, but in the Bible it says that Jesus said these things are going to happen and it's going to get worse. So for the person that doesn't have God is his life, what do you hold on to?

And, if you're afraid, as I think there's so much fear in this world today, afraid if you don't, afraid if you do, afraid if you can't, even afraid if you can, because fear is a spirit and it is the strongest of all the spirits, such as the spirit of confusion, rebellion, doubt and all kinds of spirits, but the strongest of those is the spirit of fear. If the spirit of fear can entangle you, as it did me, it grabbed me physically, tied me up where I couldn't think, started doubting, and was confused. I didn't know anything. I was lost and needed a savior. I believe that is what this world needs: a savior.

ALEXA: Wow. I wanted to ask you a question. You said something that hit home for me and brought tears to my eyes. It was very touching when you said that God works with you when you're at your lowest point or when you're in that state of fear, when you're stuck in that, when you're at the weakest point. Why do you think that?

REVEREND GARCIA: Because His Word says that. I mean, when I was in the Marine Corps, I had a manual that I had to learn, which taught all kinds of thing. Well, God has given us a manual for life. But if we don't read the manual, how would we know what to do? We're in this world fighting, not just necessarily a physical battle only because of what goes on in Afghanistan, Iraq or Vietnam, or all the other places. Isn't it interesting that it continues. It just keeps going on and on and on. It's one war after another war, after another war, after more people get killed and so forth.

I've had friends of mine die in the Vietnam War, but in the Bible it talks in Ephesians 6:13 through 17 that we're not fighting against flesh and blood, it's a spiritual warfare. So if you're not using spiritual tactics to fight the battle, you're going to get hurt. You've got to know what you're doing today. You cannot depend on anybody else. You've got to depend on what you're reading in the Bible and you've got to ask God for understanding.

We need to monitor the Bible, open the Bible up and read the Bible, and then the Bible will instruct us about everything, about what we need to do to live in this world victoriously. I live victoriously. I walk by faith. But I act on my faith, because faith without action is dead. Do you know what that means? That means that I just don't come up with an idea. I don't just pray, but once I get that clarity from God to walk and He tells me where to walk, I walk. I believe I've been inspired by God. I have learned so much, but I have so much to learn. I feel like I don't know anything.

ALEXA: That is such an amazing statement. It makes a lot of sense that life is always a learning process. There's always so much more to grow, so much more to learn, so much more faith to gain. It is a work in progress. We're always striving and working, but it's a good thing. I know we have a lot of struggles in our lives. There are different trials that God has put in our life to work through. There are a lot of blessings that come out of pain. Getting through that struggle and calling out to God is that changing point.

REVEREND GARCIA: That is how we grow. That is how we really experience knowledge and wisdom. Wisdom is something that comes from God. It's supernatural. Everyone has parents that have fathers. Well, in many cases, there are fathers that love us, that protect us, that take care of us, that teach us. There are fathers that don't do that, too, but for the most part, there are many that do and they want to protect us and teach us. That is their responsibility as a father, and also a mother.

So that is the way God is. He's our father, He's always there. He loves us more than our parents. He created us. He made us and He said, "I made you perfect in my image." When we start to have a glimpse of knowledge, of understanding, of what it is to know the love of God, we will fall to our knees and we will humble ourselves to him. We will submit. That's how it works. He wants to give us everything that He thinks we should have. That's when I pray. I pray according to His will because my will may not necessarily be good. There may be some bad things, but His will is perfect. So when I pray, I pray also that His will be done on earth as it is in heaven. That's The Lord's Prayer. He gave us the Lord's Prayer and it is universal.

It is a prayer that everyone can adapt to, but to me it's a prayer that is complete. Now there is a prayer of when you accept Jesus Christ as your Lord and Savior like in John 3 when Nicodemus came to Jesus and said, "What do you have to do to enter the kingdom of heaven?" Jesus said, "You must be born again." Nicodemus asked, "What do you mean, born again? How can I go back to my mother's womb?" Jesus replied, "I'm not talking about the spirit. I'm talking about being born in the spirit of God."

You do that when you're old enough to make a conscious decision of what you are doing. When you do that, your whole life changes. I'm telling you the way you think, the way you feel, your priorities change when you have that relationship with Jesus Christ. There is a prayer called the sinner's prayer that people are led to repeat and share and receive that prayer, but with their heart. God loves us. And right now He's here on this phone. And there are people who are hurting. They have a void in their life. They don't know what to do. They've gone to this pastor. They've gone to this priest. They've gone to this rabbi. They have gone to different people, but the void is not fixed.

So we have to come to Him humbly, like a son comes to his father and says, "Dad, I need your help and he's there to give you what you need in order to go on another day and be refreshed.

ALEXA: When we spoke previously, I was amazed and very comfortable when you said, "Let's see where God takes us. Not plan anything but let God guide the show, guide the topics, guide where it's going. It is amazing where He takes you and how He has guided this conversation so far. I feel like God has been taken out of everything and He is not involved in school. There doesn't seem to be anything sacred anymore–nothing to believe in anymore. No hope, no faith. When a person doesn't have hope or faith or something to believe in, their judgment, morals and their accountability to behave in the right way has nowhere to go.

REVEREND GARCIA: It goes exactly toward where it is right now all over the world, where there's chaos, where there's wars, where there's rumor of wars, where there's famine, where there's destruction, where children are dying. Now kids are carrying automatic weapons and they are eight or nine years old in some countries and they are killing their parents.

I believe that God knew all these things were going to happen. I believe that He's coming back. Because he has given us all free will, though, you can do whatever you want to do if that's what you want to do. I also believe, though, that there is a price that we pay for whatever we do. In other words, whatever we sow, the Bible says, we reap.

ALEXA: So true. Prayers are powerful. Personally and professionally, I have seen miracles. I can't even verbalize them. It's God. I say on a daily basis, "That's you, God, because I know I'm not capable of it and it is so powerful."

REVEREND GARCIA: And the Bible talks about Jesus saying he is not coming to bring peace, he's coming to bring a sword and causing a separation between those people that are his and those people that are not his.

ALEXA: Yes.

REVEREND GARCIA: I did a walk in Morocco from north to south and was treated like a king. It was a dangerous trip. I did a walk in Iraq, from Jordan to Iraq. I was abducted in Gaza where they are bombing today. Arafat presented me a medal in Gaza and I walked in Rafa and was abducted by two Palestinians at gunpoint because they heard that the soldiers had killed a young teenager. They were angry and I walked right into their arms. They grabbed me and threw me in a room. They intended to kill me. I said, "Jesus, I need your help. I'm in trouble." After a while they found the medal Arafat gave me and put me in a taxi. There was a crowd that was still angry and trying to turn the car over to kill me.

ALEXA: How scary.

REVEREND GARCIA: I continued to pray. I said, "Jesus, it's not over. I need your help. I need to get out of here." I prayed audibly in my spirit and all of a sudden guards with batons came from my left side and started to beat the people off the car. I saw blood from someone's head splash onto the front of the taxi windshield and heard a voice. The spirit of God said, "The blood of Jesus. You are covered by the blood of Jesus." And the car took off. It was like a movie.

ALEXA: I think many times people get caught up in debates of what people believe in and who their God is, and they fight with each other and make each other enemies, trying to get the other person to see their point while attacking their faith. It is such a distraction instead of letting people believe in what they want to believe in and being able to accept each other and have our own opinions. We can believe in our God without being attacked.

REVEREND GARCIA: I had walked from the Iwo Jima Memorial to the Capital, which took me about two to three hours. I was praying and thinking about what is going on in this world. When I got to the Capital, I sensed there is a spirit of disunity between us in our nation. We say, one nation under God, indivisible with liberty and justice for all. One God. And yet there is much bickering, arguing and fighting. I'm right. No, I'm right. No, I'm right. It's my way. No, you're wrong.

Our nation is being divided right in front of our eyes. We need to stop it. We need to stop it right now. We need to have something constructive to say. If we don't know what we're talking about we need to shut up. I'm going to be honest since you wanted me to say the truth.

ALEXA: Yes.

REVEREND GARCIA: I'm not even saying it politely because normally they say we need to be quiet, we need to shut up because there's too much talking going on, and nobody's listening, nobody's paying attention to the truth. It all belongs to God. And I have seen people die, some who die peacefully and some who fight it; they don't die peacefully. I believe that it is really important to have peace. I believe that peace is not just a matter of words; it is a matter of having a relationship with Jesus Christ. I have a relationship with Jesus Christ. I have peace. I can walk on water—I feel that by walking around the world without any money.

I have had people, sponsors, tell me that I can stay at any number of hotels—Holiday Inn, Radisson, Intercontinental or Del Coronado since God provides everything I need because He owns it all. I go directly to him in my prayers and tell Him what I need—not necessarily what I want because if I need something to eat, He provides it. If I need a place to sleep, He provides that. I've had escort vehicles of Marines and police officers around the world and you know I'm treated like a king. Well, the Bible says that I'm a priest; I'm a king. I don't drive. I haven't driven since 1996 because everywhere I've gone, I've been escorted or I've been picked up and taken where I needed to go.

Besides, God told me don't drive. Walk. Because if you drive, you're not going to walk. I pray all the time. God is the Healer. Jesus is The Healer. I'm just the vessel that He uses to pray and use words of comfort. Jesus is with them and no matter what, they shouldn't quit. Therein is the victory, when you don't quit. Often, people are so close to winning, but then quit.

ALEXA: That happens so many times. People are so close to achieving, to winning, and at that last moment they give up. It's the devil that comes in and convinces them to give up. The message is never give up.

Thank you so much for taking the time to share your story with us. Is there a way people can contact you?

REVEREND GARCIA: They can go to Globalwalk@yahoo.com. The Website is www.Globalwalk.cc. God has opened a lot of doors for me to meet a lot of people and to say thank you to them in different ways. I love all the people who are reading this. We can make a difference.

ALEXA: God bless and thank you for everything that you have done.

# Journaling Exercise

Name 5 things that you are grateful for.

Choose 5 ways that you can enhance your life mentally, emotionally, physically and spiritually.

# References

1. CBT, type of psychotherapy in which negative patterns of thought about the self and the world are challenged in order to alter unwanted behavior patterns or treat mood disorders such as depression.

2. National Alliance on Mental Illness https://www.nami.org/

3. Short Term Couples Therapy The Imago Model In Action, second edition, by Wade Luquet Foreword by Harville Hendrix, 2007, Routledge Taylor and Francis Group

4. Mirroring means repeating back your partner's words so you both know you have actually heard the Sender's words. Both the Sender and the Receiver have responsibilities during Mirroring. http://www.relationshipjourney.com/dialoguetipsdawn.html

5. Detaching From Emotional Pain. (Grounding), Guilford Press, NY, from: Najavits. LM "Seeking Safety" A Treatment Manual For PTSD and Substance Abuse ( in Press)

CPSIA information can be obtained at www.ICGtesting.com
Printed in the USA
LVOW07s2310110916

504188LV00001B/79/P